Light the World

How Your Brilliance Can Shift the Planet

by Marnie L. Pehrson

Copyright 2012 Marnie L. Pehrson
All Rights Reserved

Cover Design by Sheri Brady
http://www.behance.net/mightyphoenix

Published by Spirit Tree Publishing
514 Old Hickory Ln * Ringgold GA 30736
Tel: 706-866-2295
www.SpiritTreePublishing.com

ISBN: 978-0-9825878-4-3
Library of Congress: 2012910652

Dedication

First, I'd like to dedicate this book to my father. I can imagine God deciding He wanted to create an entrepreneur who helped Light Bearers lead this world to freedom. Perhaps he asked himself, "Who would be the perfect father for this individual?" If such a thing happened, I have no doubt that His answer would have been "Jack Morton." There is no way to enumerate all the ways my father prepared me for my life's work. I love you, Daddy!

Next, I dedicate this to my friends in the Light the World group who came together like an old barn-raising to make this book a reality. I couldn't have done it without y'all!

TABLE OF CONTENTS

What Is a Light Bearer? 1
Why Light Bearers Matter: The Coming World-Shift 9
The Parable of the Quartz 17
Phase 1: Formed Under Intense Heat and Pressure . 23
Phase 2: Mined 33
Phase 3: White 41
Phase 4: Clear 57
Phase 5: Transparent 67
Phase 6: Refraction, Resonance, and Healing 81
As a Man Thinketh 87
You Are the Creator of Your Own Life 97
You Are a Healer 117
Building Your Tribe 121
Lamp Bearers 129
Advocates and Thought Leaders 133
7 Ways to Create a World-Changing Movement .. 143
Destined for Freedom 151
About the Author 159

ACKNOWLEDGEMENTS

I'd like to thank the Lord for bringing all the elements for this book together in perfect synchronicity. As a result, it was the fastest book I've ever put in print.

On the other hand, I feel like I've spent a decade gathering the information for it without really knowing what I was doing. The big picture remained elusive until I read Oliver DeMille's *FreedomShift: 3 Choices to Reclaim America's Destiny*. Then, it was as if someone put the final piece to a puzzle in place, and suddenly everything made sense.

On the heels of reading DeMille's book, my friend Laura West invited me to participate in her 30-Day Passion Project Program (PassionProjectsAlive.com/30day). Laura encouraged me to focus specifically on the project that fueled my passion most. With my big vision securely in place, the timing was perfect to work on this book.

Once committed, a wonderful group of Light Bearers rallied around to make it a reality.

A big thanks to Alysia Humphries and JoAnna Ashley for finding the front cover photo. Love it!

After a call for stories, the following individuals responded within 48 hours with their heart-felt stories that added richness to the book: Joyce Pierce, James Moore, JoAnna Ashley, Martina Muir, Miko Batty,

Daryl O'Bryant, Pamela Stevens-Steffensen, Carolyn Cooper, Amy Oliver, Liz King Bradley, Victoria Fielding, Carolyn Murphy, Lisa Rae Preston, Leslie Householder, Denise Webster, and Pamela Stevens-Steffensen.

All of the aforementioned individuals as well as April Hennis, Dr. Joseph Peck, David Perdew, and Judy Hansen provided valuable input on the cover and title.

A special thanks to fast readers who gave overnight input: Laila Ellis Kammerman, Martina Muir, Denise Webster, Jonelle Rust Hughes, Lorna Stirewalt Morrison, and JoAnna Ashley. And I often wonder if I could ever write a decent back cover copy without the talented Lisa Rae Preston.

As always, it's a pleasure to work with my editor, Meredith Dias (MeredithDias.com), and my talented book designer, Sheri Brady (behance.net/mightyphoenix). It's wonderful knowing I can count on quality, timely work from these professionals.

Finally, I'd like to express my gratitude to my wonderful friends and family members who have spent hours brainstorming ideas and being my sounding boards. You've listened to me rattle on without ever once telling me my dreams are crazy or my vision for lighting the world is impossible. Rather, many of you have stepped up and joined me on my journey. I love you all and you know who you are!

What Is a Light Bearer?

Had someone asked me what my message was prior to February 2012, I would have told them that my message is that YOU have a message. I firmly believe each individual is here to share a message. Some do it proactively by writing books, speaking, teaching, or consulting. Others radiate their message in the way they live their lives. It's just who they are.

I believe that, as disciples of Christ, we especially are here to share a message that God has planted within us. Your message is unique to you. You reflect Christ's light in a way that only you can.

Jesus said:

Ye are the light of the world. A city that is set on an hill cannot be hid. Neither do men light a candle, and put it under a bushel, but on a candlestick; and it giveth light unto all that are in the house.

Let your light so shine before men, that they may see your good works, and glorify your Father which is in heaven. (Matthew 5:14-16)

This is a foundational belief for me. I love helping people find that light within themselves, shine it out for others to see, and be blessed as a result.

Even though I was passionate about helping others discover, cultivate, and share their messages, I often became discontent, feeling as if something was missing. You may know that feeling: You're close, but you haven't quite found your sweet spot.

I was praying about this in February 2012, and the answer came very clearly to me: "Telling other people that they have a message is NOT your message. You have your own message. Take out a pen and paper and figure out what it is. Once you have that, you will have your focus and you will stay passionate about what you do."

I started writing as instructed, and a list of people came to me. On this list were people who have made an impact on my life. They're individuals with whom I resonate, who have taught me valuable truths, inspired me, and taught me to love. I came up with a list of twenty individuals, six of whom are my own children.

Then, I wrote next to each person's name what I love about them, what inspires me about them. As I did this, I began to see a pattern. Right off the bat, I saw a common theme of liberty. Each has taught me about some aspect of freedom, including:

- Freedom to Create
- Freedom to Change/Break Free of Bondage
- Owning Your Own Power and Respecting Other People's Right to Own Theirs
- Freedom of Expression
- Freedom to Love without Limits

I was floored. I had no idea that I was being drawn to people with this common thread. It's actually quite ironic, because if someone had asked who symbolized freedom in my life, I would have said my father. "Freedom" is my father's favorite chord on the keyboard of life, and he's been telling me for forty-plus years that it's not just a chord, but a refrain that weaves through every song—at least any song worth singing.

I would say, "Yeah, yeah, I see what you mean." I did see what he meant, but I was really thinking, "It's just your pet subject, Daddy." To me, freedom was my father's message, not mine! Yet there it was, an underlying soundtrack in all my relationships, connecting the plotline of my life, actions, and results.

Over the course of four days, I studied the common characteristics and threads in my twenty people even more and discovered what they symbolize to me.

As I did this, two things happened:

- I gained a deeper understanding of who I am and what my own message is. What we see and admire in others is what exists in ourselves.
- I came away with a clearer description of the typical person I'm passionate about serving.

Here's what I uncovered about both who I am and who I serve. I call it being a Light Bearer. If you're reading this book, I suspect you are one!

Light Bearers Defined

- Courageous creatives who choose to be conduits of charity (aka pure love).
- Leaders who stand for life, liberty, learning, love, and beauty.

So here's my official definition of a Light Bearer:

A Light Bearer is a wise, intuitive inspired creative who lovingly lights the way for others. A Light Bearer is passionate about assisting people in breaking free from bondage to attain ultimate freedom (whether the chains are of one's own making, generational, or inflicted by others). Light Bearers are courageous leaders for not only the rising generation but also for lifelong learners of any age.

Upon discovering this common thread among the people I love to work with and who have impacted my life, I decided to focus more proactively on assisting Light Bearers in any way possible. I vowed to be a more courageous Light Bearer myself and to continue to work synergistically with my fellow Light Bearers.

> *The Spirit of the Lord God is upon me; because the Lord hath anointed me to preach good tidings unto the meek; he hath sent me to bind up the brokenhearted, to proclaim liberty to the captives, and the opening of the prison to them that are bound.* (Isaiah 61:1)

While Isaiah spoke of the Messiah with this verse, and Jesus quoted it as He began His mortal ministry (Luke 4:18), I believe that, as disciples of Christ, we have the same calling. We are His hands and feet to preach good, to bind up the brokenhearted, and proclaim liberty to the captives. Because of Christ's light shining through us, through our example and wisdom, we can liberate those who are imprisoned.

Find Your Own Message

Are you still wondering what your message is? Try this exercise for yourself. Write down the names of the people you admire most, who have impacted your life. You don't even have to know them personally. Then write next to their names what you love and admire most about them.

Then look for the common threads and themes. I put my people's photos in columns and rows and rearranged them until I started to see commonalities. For example, my matrix has five rows:

- **Row 1:** Courageous advocates of truth.
- **Row 2:** Inspired creatives who think outside the box.
- **Row 3:** Individuals who've taught me about respecting other people's freedom to choose and how to help people without encroaching upon their agency.
- **Row 4:** Lifelong learners who express themselves in beautiful, creative ways, particularly through music.
- **Row 5:** Glowing balls of love. For these folks, love seems to have no limits, and others are magnetically drawn to them as a result.

There are other common threads going down the columns. The more I look at my matrix, the more insights I gain about the people I love to serve and long to be. Using the words and attributes I discovered from the matrix, I composed my definition of Light Bearers.

Here are the steps to try it yourself:

1) Make a list of the people you admire, who have impacted your life for good, or with whom you resonate. You don't have to know all of these people personally. For example, I had one person on my list I greatly admire, but whom I've never personally met or interacted with in any way.
2) To the right of each name, jot down the characteristics you admire in these individuals. Also, write any positive themes they represent to you or lessons they've taught you.
3) Once you've done this for everyone on the list, go back and look for patterns in the words and descriptors you've used. Do you see the same words or phrases coming up with several people?
4) Jot down those words. Most likely, these characteristics or themes lie within you. You may readily see some of these in yourself. Others may feel like wishful thinking. Know that within you lies each characteristic or theme. You can set goals around these characteristics to further develop these traits.
5) The words you've discovered represent the people you like to be around and probably would like to work with. This can help you in deciding what types of people to add to your life, what types of clients or customers you want to seek, or what types of relationships you want to foster.
6) If you want, you can go a step further and create your own matrix. Take each of the characteristics or themes you found repeated in your list. Write

those down the left-hand side of a piece of paper. Next to those words, write the names (from left to right) of the people who possessed these characteristics. You can put these in a table. Feel free to play with it and shuffle people around. Look for patterns. There's no "right" way to do this. As you do this, you may find further insights like I did. Give it a try! It's a fun, enlightening experience.

Why Light Bearers Matter: The Coming World-Shift

Come with me to South Carolina during the Revolutionary War. Young Dicey Langston (www.DiceyLangston.com) is fifteen years old. She lives in a district of the state that predominantly supports the British (also called Loyalists). Yet her brothers fight for the Patriot cause, and her father was wounded in battle fighting for America's freedom.

While mingling amidst her neighbors, she often overhears Loyalist plans to harass Patriots or even attack their settlements. No one pays much attention to a young girl, so they don't guard their words around her. Thus, she is able to overhear important information and carry it to her brothers. She carries so many messages that eventually a ruthless band of Loyalists known as the "Bloody Scouts" catches on to what she's doing and warns her father to take control of his "feisty, meddlesome daughter," or they will take care of him and his family. When the Bloody Scouts take care of you, you are as good as dead and your house is looted and burned.

Thus, Dicey's father warns her to cease her activities for the family's safety. Not long after this, Dicey overhears that the "Bloody Scouts" are going to attack the Elder settlement at Little Eden, South Carolina, at dawn. Her brother James is stationed at this settlement. Knowing she can't inform her father and trusting no one else with the message, Dicey sets out on foot in the middle of the night, crosses a swollen river, and nearly drowns. Finally, she makes it to the Elder Settlement in time to warn her brother James so that he and his men can alert the settlement. When the Bloody Scouts arrive the next morning, the Elder Settlement has been evacuated.

On multiple occasions, Dicey courageously faced the enemy; she even saved her father by throwing herself in front of him when he was held at gunpoint by the Bloody Scouts. Her courage and patriotism have inspired me greatly as her fourth great-granddaughter. She has taught me much about the difference that one person can make. One individual can change the world for the better and affect lives for centuries to come. Thousands honor Dicey as their grandmother and can trace their roots back to her through one of her twenty-two children. Not only that, but everyone descended from the survivors of the Elder settlement owe their very existence to this fifteen-year-old girl.

During the Revolutionary War, only about 3 percent of the population was actively involved in the fight for freedom. The rest either didn't care or were for the British. Perhaps this is why Samuel Adams said, "It does not require a majority to prevail, but rather an irate, tireless minority keen to set brush fires in people's minds."

As a Light Bearer you can be among those who set brush fires in people's hearts and minds!

A friend sent me a CD called Freedom Matters by Oliver DeMille (www.oliverdemille.com). In it he talks about a coming world shift. Approximately every century, a nation makes a shift either toward freedom or toward force. In 1776 we had a Freedom Shift in America. Between 1913 and 1936, we experienced a Force Shift with the implementation of the federal income tax, the Federal Reserve, the change in the election of senators, and the redefinition of the general welfare clause.

DeMille has studied nations and the last 3,000 years of history, and says we're in line for a coming shift—on a world scale rather than just a national one due to the increasingly global nature of our technological society.

Will we experience a force shift or a freedom shift? The momentum, DeMille claims, is toward a force shift. But he also says there's much hope for a freedom shift. In any shift, 95 to 97 percent of the people are not even involved. They simply don't care. This leaves 3 to 5 percent of the populace to make things happen, and that number is split between the people wanting more force and those wanting more freedom. So, in essence, if we want a Freedom Shift, we only need to comprise about 2.5 percent of the population.

Seems doable—especially given the rising interest in liberty in this country. DeMille says that three important choices must be made by 2.5 percent of the population in order to insure a Freedom Shift.

1) **We need more entrepreneurs.** Historically, nations with a solid base of entrepreneurs experience freedom. If force is imposed on them, it doesn't last long. Entrepreneurship and government oppression do not coexist -- at least not long-term.
2) **We need more voracious readers and independent thinkers** involved in the fight for freedom. You can't be a nation of sheep believing everything you see in the media or read in tabloids and be free for long. People who read voraciously tend to think more independently and thus value freedom more.
3) **We need more tribal leaders.** A tribal leader is someone who leads other people with similar interests. But tribes go beyond interests and niches. DeMille explains, "When your relationships with one person or more in a given niche reach the point that you deeply care about these people, and they about you, you are part of a new tribe" (Oliver DeMille, *FreedomShift: 3 Choices to Reclaim America's Destiny*, Kindle Location 2105).

What I loved about the CD is that it explained so much about what I've been feeling the compulsion to do for the last decade: to help build entrepreneurs and to foster and promote thought leaders (aka tribal leaders).

I believe it's critical that Light Bearers see the big picture of where we're going and what we're doing to impact the world. If you're reading this, you have a desire to change the world. You may have a message, a truth, or a system that you feel compelled to share. Perhaps you're so excited about what other people are coming up with that you are learning from various thought leaders. You're piecing things together.

I want to assist you as a Light Bearer to understand what's happening on a global scale. This is what has come to me through research, experience, and study. You may see some metaphors that sound familiar or you may not. It's exciting to see what is happening on this planet. In this book, I'll be sharing what I've learned so far, and I hope you'll share with me what you're seeing as well. I know there's more to this picture, and I'm always open to learning from new people, ideas, and perspectives.

Let me relate an analogy that will convey what I believe is happening in the world today and why Light Bearers are so significant.

Imagine, if you will, a tree in an open meadow. This tree has white, sweet, beautiful fruit on it. The tree represents the love of God. On the other side of the field is a large and spacious building with ornate doors and lots of windows. It's floating midair. This building represents the pride of the world. It includes the philosophies of men and everything men have come up with to achieve power and gain.

Next, imagine a path meandering through a winding wilderness terrain that leads to the tree. Alongside this path is a rod of iron that one can hang onto to stay on the path. It represents the Word of God. There are mists of darkness that weave across the path, making it difficult to see or to travel. There are also side roads where someone could get lost—that might take them over cliffs, onto jagged rocks, or over to the spacious building.

This is a metaphor for what is happening in the world today. There are people on the path leading to the tree who are trying to decide where to go. Some people are getting lost in mists of darkness and sidetracked onto dangerous paths. Others are seeing the building and heading off toward it with great purpose and direction.

Still others hold to the rod of iron (Word of God) and stay on the path. Others get lax, let go of the iron rod, and slip off into the mist of darkness.

I'd heard this metaphor many times in my life, but a few years ago, I had an insight about it. It was as if the Lord were saying to me, "The people along the path and in the wilderness cannot see Me. But they can see you." The mists of darkness are obstructing their view, and they can't see Christ or the tree. But they can see you and me! So, what if there are people along this path holding on to the rod with one hand and lifting a lamp with the other? What if there are kind souls lighting the way, illuminating the path?

All along the path, there are people saying, "Stay on this path. Go to the tree, not to the building. The building is going to fall. It's hanging up in the air and eventually it will fall. It lacks a sure foundation."

So these Light Bearers are who we are. We are holding up a light saying, "Go to the tree. Don't go to the building." But other people are using a lot of the same tools that we use (like law of attraction, law of cause and effect, energy work, etc.). The tools are good. They are useful, but like any tool (like television or the internet) they can be used for good or evil. There are other people set out along the path and in the mists of darkness who are using these tools to guide people to the building. Using these tools, they show people how to go after the pride of their hearts, to seek power and gain—all of which are overflowing from the great and spacious building. These people often use force (or governments) to accomplish their objectives.

So while the Light Bearers use tools to lead people to the love of God, other people use them to guide people to the pride of the world.

It doesn't take many Light Bearers to change the world. It may be the 2.5 percent that Oliver DeMille mentioned, or it may be even less. If you look at the story of Gideon in the Old Testament, you see that God only needs a small number of people to work a miracle. Gideon had gathered an army to fight the Midianites and the Amalekites. God told him he had too many people and to tell any who were afraid to go home. Twenty-two thousand people left, leaving ten thousand.

At this point, the Lord told Gideon he still had too many. The people came to a body of water, and the Lord told Gideon to divide the people who got down and lapped the water up like a dog from the people who knelt and lifted the water in their hands to drink. He told Gideon to send home the ones who lapped it up and keep the remaining. This left three hundred men to go against the nations of the Midianites and Amalekites. Through miraculous means, Gideon's three hundred (1 percent of his original army) were able to defeat them.

Note the two characteristics of the people through whom the Lord chose to work His miracle: They were fearless and they were alert. These two characteristics are significant when we set our feet on the path to being a Light Bearer. It takes courage to put yourself out there, to be different, and to stand with integrity in the face of opposition. It also means we have to wake up and see things that the masses do not see. Being alert and aware are key characteristics of Light Bearers.

As we develop these characteristics, we may be few, but with the Lord on our side, we can work miracles!

The Parable of the Quartz

In December 2009, two friends and I met in Zion National Park, intent upon creating a four-day event called "Light the World: Birthing Your Destiny" and sharing the process of becoming a Light Bearer. Our objective was to take a group of women through the process that I had discovered for reflecting God's light to the world.

To illustrate the process, I stepped into a rock shop and asked the clerk if she had any stones that went from white to clear and then transparent as they were processed, cut, or shaped. She directed me to quartz. She handed me a fist-size chunk. It was white with a few tan blemishes. Jagged and imperfect, one would never guess that it had the potential to be completely transparent. Then she handed me a few pieces of cut quartz. In fingerlike slices, the quartz had now become clear—imperfect still, but clear. Finally, she showed me a bin full of round smooth, transparent stones. These glasslike orbs could easily be placed in a light box to reflect light into a room.

Quartz can also be cut into prisms, which refract an entire rainbow of colors and bring beauty into the world.

The shopkeeper also shared with us the healing properties of quartz. Clear quartz is known as the "master healer." It's believed to amplify energy, spirituality, and thought. It even stimulates the immune system and creates balance in the body. Rose quartz is believed to open the heart to unconditional love and improve relationships.

As my friends and I moved forward with the Light the World Retreat, we took this theme and wove it through the entire event. Day one was about becoming White, day two was about becoming Clear, day three about becoming Transparent, and day four about Shining. It was remarkable to watch this theory bearing fruit in our participants' lives. By the end of the event, these ladies were on fire with the Light of Christ, and clear about who they are and what they are on this planet to do. The process worked! I believe it was more about the setting and the environment than anything we did. These women were willing to put themselves in this place of unconditional love and acceptance where they could be transformed. The end result? God changed them!

When we set a clear intention to be a conduit of Christ's light to the world and step into an environment that supports that, God can then transform us into the people He knows we can become. The ultimate product is a life of light, joy, and abundance.

As Christians, our greatest achievement is to be a reflection of His light and love to others. It is in Him and through Him that we find our bliss.

> "Men and women who turn their lives over to God will discover that He can make a lot more

out of their lives than they can." —Ezra Taft Benson

The 6 Phases of Quartz

There's something about knowing the Light Bearer Cycle (the Parable of the Quartz) and where you are in that cycle that brings peace and clarity. As I mentioned earlier, it takes courage to be a Light Bearer. Your vision will often be seen as impractical to others—even impractical to yourself! Other people may think you're a dreamer or downright crazy. But the truth is, "where there is no vision, people perish" (Proverbs 29:18).

Gaining clarity about where you are along this path will help you understand that what's happened in the past and what's happening in the present is all for a reason. You'll also know what to look for in the future. It will give you hope that things will work out, that you're actually moving toward a wonderful, illuminated place.

So let's take a closer look at the Light Bearer process by studying the Parable of the Quartz.

Phase 1: Formed Under Intense Heat and Pressure
Not all quartz is crystallized. In order to become crystallized, quartz must undergo extreme pressure and heat.

Phase 2: Mined
Quartz is taken from the earth and mined, cut, or hewn. At this point, it may have impurities—some dark spots, some white, and even some clear spots.

Phase 3: White
As you cut the quartz, it can become very white and beautiful.

Phase 4: Clear
As you further cut the quartz, you'll create more clarity.

Phase 5: Transparent
The more heat, pressure, and cutting a piece of quartz goes through, the more likely it can become transparent like glass.

Phase 6: Refraction, Resonance, and Healing
Eventually, crystallized quartz can become prismatic, refracting white light into a myriad of colors and sending it sparkling in all directions. As I mentioned earlier, many also believe that quartz crystals have healing and spiritual properties.

Quartz is also capable of steady vibrations (called oscillations) that can be used to regulate electricity. This makes it useful in clocks and computers.

The same process used to shape quartz is reflected in our own lives. Adversity and life experiences slice through us, helping us to cut away the impurities and reveal our clear purpose. Like the quartz crystals, you can become a reflection (or refraction) of God's light to the world. As you go through this process, you will have a healing influence on those around you and bring balance to the planet.

Just like quartz, Light Bearers emit a "steady vibration" that empowers and liberates the world. There are so many people who have no sense of direction, no moorings. They are lost, and the steady vibration of a Light Bearer (who has "been there, done that") is exactly what they need to help them find their way out of captivity and into freedom.

In the next few chapters, we'll delve into the process of becoming a reflection of Christ's light to the world. I hope you'll join me on this grand adventure. Let's look at those six phases again from the perspective of your life and being a Light Bearer.

Resource: "Quartz Mining," The Encyclopedia of Arkansas History & Culture, http://encyclopediaofarkansas.net/encyclopedia/entry-detail.aspx?entryID=1173

Phase 1: Formed Under Intense Heat and Pressure

My friend Joyce Pierce, author of Saving Nikki (www.SavingNikki.com), encapsulates how the intense pressure of life shaped her destiny.

> My parents loved each other and couldn't wait to start a life together, but before long, alcohol took control of their lives and they lost everything that was dear to them. They divorced, and at the age of seven, I went to live with my grandparents. My father remarried about three years later and my mother left the state, believing that we would have a better life without her. My father found a new wife but I definitely didn't gain a mother.
>
> At sixteen I was drawn to a young man who simply paid attention to me. He was charming, said all the right things, and I believed all of it. By the time I realized how much of a hold he had on me, it was too late. Married and pregnant before I graduated from high school, I didn't realize the consequences that would result from my choices. Because of pride, I endured an abusive relationship with someone who wasn't committed to me, and before our second child was born, it was over.

He left me without a car, without a paycheck, and without a husband in the delivery room. Alone in that hospital at 19, I committed to creating a better life for myself and my children. I found a job, bought a car, and with each success, have come to appreciate my self worth. I have shared my story of hope through my novel, Saving Nikki, and am strengthened by the comments from women whose hearts have been touched. Because I understand how frightening it can be to have life dumped in your lap, I have also worked to help thousands of men and women record information that will be helpful to their loved ones in their absence. It's not uncommon to feel abandoned when a loved one dies, but when they loved you enough to leave you instructions for how to carry on without them, it's a real treasure that will give you comfort as you deal with your loss.

Almost all Light Bearers have been through challenges that have put intense heat or pressure on them. Some may have caused their own challenges through unwise choices or self-harm. Others may have been pressurized externally by illness, abuse, financial challenges, etc. There are some who have no "wounded healer" story, but have spent many years helping other people (children, spouses, family members, or clients) through their challenges.

No one on this planet is immune to challenges. It is how we respond to those challenges that determines whether we are crushed or made into a beautiful crystal.

Denise Webster of AllAboutBecoming.com shared this story. I feel it holds significance in our discussion of the intense pressure Light Bearers endure and transcend.

> In Sunday school, we were talking about the parable of the 10 Virgins and how it relates to us. I've heard it said that the oil in our lamps is our testimonies, and that is why we cannot "share" our oil with others. Our teacher mentioned olive oil was used to light the lamps and how much effort went into producing the olive oil. In my mind, I thought of the process of making olive oil. We have heard it used in symbolism with Gethsemane. Here is an explanation by David Ridges in his book, *The New Testament Made Easier*.
>
>> *The word Gethsemane means oil press. There is significant symbolism here. The Jews put olives into bags made of mesh fabric and placed them in a press to squeeze olive oil out of them. The first pressings yielded pure olive oil which was prized for many uses, including healing and giving light in lanterns. In fact, we consecrate it and use it to administer to the sick. The last pressing of the olives, under the tremendous pressure of additional weights added to the press, yielded a bitter, red liquid which can remind us of the "bitter cup" which the Savior partook of. Symbolically, the Savior is going into the "oil press" (Gethsemane) to*

> *submit to the "pressure" of all our sins which will "squeeze" His blood out in order that we might have the healing "oil" of the Atonement to heal us from our sins.*

It is the intense pressure that extracts the oil and gives us the purest oil. If we think of this symbolically in our lives, then it is the pressure (the struggles and challenges) that we go through that extract the best in us—that makes us pure, creates our oil, and makes us pure enough to see Christ. THIS is the reason we cannot "share" our oil. Our trials are our own. It is through overcoming them and becoming pure that we have "oil" and we cannot share that. Each person must go through this individually. The trials and challenges we go through are truly blessings. It is the Lord's way of purging the impurities from our souls and creating a pureness so that we will be able to stand in His presence and live with Him again. When I see someone going through a trial, I often think they must be special because the Lord is giving them a gift and helping them create oil for their lamps.

Note that the second pressing creates a bitter red oil. When we continue to press and press on our own problems and struggles, like calling friends or family and hashing and discussing and complaining and continually talking about our problems/issues, then we can create bitterness in our own lives. I've done this, so I know. I usually can talk myself through a problem, but when I call someone or somebody asks me, then I can get heated up, worked up, and re-wrapped up in an issue. The secret is to not keep pressing and creating bitterness, but to use the struggle or trial to create purity. Let it fill our lamps and move on.

My friend Martina Muir's (MartinaMuir.com) story conveys important themes you'll find common among many Light Bearers.

> When I was young, I had horrible self worth. I couldn't stand to be in my own skin. I constantly beat myself up verbally and even harmed myself physically for many years. Because I hated myself so badly, I surrounded myself with people and environments that treated me poorly, too. I ended up having a baby at age 17. My boyfriend at the time was heavily into gangs, drugs, and alcohol. I wanted my child to have a loving home with two parents and I knew that would not be possible with the environments he would be exposed to if I raised my son. I chose to place him for adoption. It was one of the most painful experiences of my life! But it was also one of the most rewarding. I KNEW without a shadow of a doubt that I was doing a selfless and amazing act of love. Because I loved my son so much, I sacrificed my desires to give him more. When I handed him to his new parents I felt an instant connection and love for them. It was because of my sacrifice that I was able to witness the beginning of a new family; my

beloved son with loving parents who had longed to have children for many years.

Grieving and healing after you place for adoption is a long and painful road. I still never regretted the decision, but that did not diminish the pain. Twelve years went by. I still thought of him often and it did get easier with time, but it wasn't until 2007 that I truly got the healing I had been craving for so long.

So what changed in 2007?

I started to get a burning feeling inside. I could feel deep within that there was something I needed to accomplish on this planet. There were people that needed my help. I started to volunteer at the local adoption agency with other birthmoms who were going through what I had 12 years earlier. I connected with these girls and shared the things that I had been doing to help me through the hard times.

However, I was extremely surprised to find that I was the one who was finding deeper healing. Each week I would come home with a very full heart. My heart was cracked open and the pain was being healed through the service I gave to these beautiful young women. As my buried emotions were brought to the surface, I found it extremely painful for the first 3 months. Oftentimes I would come home and sob for hours.

One night as I was desperately crying out in prayer to have relief from the overwhelming emotions, I asked the question "Why do I have to share these painful memories?"

These words came to my mind: "This experience is no longer yours."

From that night on, I began to understand that as we learn and grow from the painful experiences in our lives, at some point it no longer belongs to us and we need to share it with others. It is our duty to help those who may be suffering from the same things we have gone through.

Another individual whose story has inspired me belongs to Daryl O'Bryant, cross-country runner and blogger (Sub4Minds.com). Notice how Daryl overcame adversity, found the lesson, and is proactively inspiring others to share in his discoveries.

> I come from a running family. Most of my brothers and my sister all ran track and/or cross country. Some were able to use running as the means for a college education. Running was a common, everyday kind of thing in our home.
> When I was a teenager, my father announced that he was going to do a virtual run across the United States. We all thought it was kind of cool, different, and exciting. None of us ever doubted that it was doable. Still, this was quite an undertaking. Much more so in the days before Google, the internet, or any other technology. Armed with a road atlas, paper, pencil, and a ruler, my Dad created a log and hit the road. On any given day, he could tell you his current location, a little bit of the geography, and upcoming milestone destinations.

Fast forward to 2005, when a fall from my roof left me with a broken neck (three fractures on C3 and C4) and a broken wrist. Sometime after the accident I found myself at a playground with my family. I watched children running and playing. I heard the happy sounds of their unrestrained excitement. In that moment, I understood the source of their happiness and laughter. The children on the playground found sheer joy in just running, jumping, sliding . . . The simple act of movement made them happy. I realized that Movement Is Life!

I began running again. Very slowly at first. I began to set and achieve mild running goals. As time went on I began to set higher and somewhat more aggressive goals.

Then, in the summer of 2011, I was in a car accident. My second night in ICU, I was lying awake and thinking about the next few months of my life and what I would get to experience. While tethered to that hospital bed, I remembered the lesson learned at that playground 6 years earlier. I made the firm decision that I would not sit and wait for recovery to happen. I would be proactive in helping my body to mend itself. At the same, I would respect my body's need to rest and recover. But I would be moving! And living!

I set cautious, but assertive goals at first. I used this time to listen to my body, being sure to give it room to heal itself. Slowly, as I regained my strength (and at my doctor's encouragement) I set higher goals. Within 5 months of the accident, I had surpassed my pre-accident Personal Bests!

I began to realize that, with a little focus, hard work, and determination, I am capable of doing much more than I had ever imagined. With that latest bit of self-discovery fresh in my mind, I started looking for a fun new BIG goal. Somewhere in the search, I remembered my father's great coast-to-coast run.

I encourage you to follow along with Daryl's virtual run across the country on his blog at Sub4Minds.com.

What is your story? What adversities and challenges have you overcome? Whenever I consult with clients, I encourage them to lead with their story. There are literally thousands of life coaches, business consultants, internet marketers, authors, and speakers. What makes you unique, and what will encourage others to choose to work with you instead of someone else, is YOUR STORY! Don't be afraid to share it. Your story resonates!

Phase 2: Mined

You are a collection of talents, gifts, and God-given divinity. You're also a collection of life experiences, traumas, flaws, and human frailties. All these things have come together to make you who you are. You aren't perfect, and that's okay. You're a beautiful creation of God. Along the way you've learned some wonderful things—how to overcome trials and challenges. You can be a light to help others cross their wildernesses of darkness.

Along this journey, at some point you're "set aside" or taken out of the world in some way. You may feel like you're different. You may feel a yearning or a "call" to help others. You know that there is something unique about you. You have been "set apart" for something more.

Some people remember one defining moment when they felt "called" to step up to the plate and make a difference. Others have had this "knowing" that they are destined for something significant for as long as they can remember. I'll share with you examples of each.

Carolyn Cooper, the creator of the Carolyn Cooper SimplyHealed Method(R) (CarolynCooper.com) shares the moment when she answered the "call" to step out and light the world in the way she's uniquely qualified to do.

Before I began instructing others in my SimplyHealed™ Method, I took private clients. There were some days when I would get lots of people with really heavy issues. Although I knew my method could help them, it saddened me to see all the dysfunction in the world that children have grown up with in their families. I kept having the prompting for about a year, "Write a manual and teach this so that other people can learn to do it."

I was very reluctant to follow this prompting because I thought it would be too hard for me to explain how I do what I do. Since a lot of it is intangible I didn't know if I could articulate it well enough for people to really 'get' it. I also wondered if people would actually want to come to my classes. I was teaching some other energy classes—not quite as advanced as SimplyHealed™. I was teaching simpler things, giving hour-long lectures and little workshops. But I kept putting off the inspiration to teach the full method.

One day I was driving home. I had worked at Red Mountain Spa for two days straight, about 9 sessions in a row each day. An appointment is an hour long, so that's a lot when it's issues of grief, loss, and trauma that I'm working on with clients. In a way, it's not that sad to me in fact, it's actually very rewarding work because I know my method of emotional clearing will help them heal from these things. But at the same time, I was exhausted. I was driving home from that second day, and I felt drained. I was talking to God in my mind saying, "There is so much negativity and abuse in the world. I'm grateful for this gift. I know it really helps people, but I'm one person doing this work, and I am also a wife and a mother of five. I know there are light workers out there in the world, but it seems like the ratio of light workers (energy practitioners and healers) to the darkness in the world, is so unbalanced."

I was pouring my heart out to God when I heard in my mind clearly the words, "That's why I'm asking you to teach others." Whoa. I finally got it! It was only about one week later that I had my first class scheduled and was getting the word out. I had quite a few people signed up even before I had a manual written. I got the manual written, and since that time hundreds of students have been through my course. It's so much fun to teach people how to help themselves and others.

I get emails from them about ways they've been able to help friends, family, and clients of their own. It makes me cry to think just how much joy this brings me and how happy I am to be able to do it. It's wonderful to know these people are out there helping others and changing their lives for the better.

Denise Webster of AllAboutBecoming.com shares the moment she gained her vision of what was possible for her and how it brought clarity about her message.

In October 2008, I attended a Mentor Training with Leslie Householder. At one point she used a visualization technique that helped us discover our purpose. I was totally clueless about mine. We were paired with a partner. We were to close our eyes while Leslie talked to us and we pictured in our minds the things she told us.

She started by telling us to picture a stage and a large group of people who were very excited to hear the message that was to be given. I was picturing a stage with a lot of people, kind of like a concert. Then she told us there was a microphone, and we were the ones who would be speaking. My mind shifted to our high school auditorium with the black flooring, black curtains, totally empty except for a single microphone in the center of the stage. My mind went there because I had just spent hours and hours in the auditorium working on the set for the school play my son was in.

I pictured myself walking up to this microphone on the empty stage. I stopped myself and thought, *"What am I doing here? What am I supposed to do? Am I a stand-up comedian? No. Am I supposed to sing like my son? No. Well, what am I doing and why am I here?"* Just as that thought finished from the right to the left a new screen came up. It was a huge auditorium with a stage at the front. My very next thought was "What in the WORLD am I doing HERE?"

Leslie's voice then cut in..."You are looking out into your audience. Who do you see?" My picture took me behind the microphone. There were spotlights shining on me, and I looked out into this vast crowd sitting in dimmed lights. There were lots of people. I started to cry—physically, right there. My partner asked me if I was okay. I told her I was just overwhelmed at what I was seeing. Then Leslie continued, "You are beginning to speak. What message are you giving them?"

At that instant I saw a shaft of light some straight from the ceiling dropping down on the top of my head. As I spoke, the light went from my mouth and shot out to the crowd in a fan, filling the room. I said to them, "God loves you." Tears were streaming down my face because not only could I see it, but I could FEEL it. I FELT this overwhelming, powerful, unexplainable love that God has for each of us. My poor partner—she didn't know what to do. I was overcome with so much emotion.

My mind began racing again: *"What does this mean? Is this what I am supposed to do? Will I really be standing in front of thousands of people? If so, I am NOT even close to being the kind of person I would need to be to speak to an audience of this magnitude. I would need great character and integrity."* It scared me and yet it also put something in my heart that this was the type of person I was capable of being. Everything in me changed that day. I had a new direction and purpose for who I was to truly become.

As I came home understanding that this new really good person was inside me, all desires for things that were not good left me. I was shocked at how when you have a direction and focus on who you truly are as a son or daughter of God, that the desire to have anything to do with the world in your life dissipates. You no longer are on that level or wavelength, and you desire and YEARN for something higher, better, and eternal.

I learned that as soon as I had a purpose and a mission for what I was to accomplish (and mine is to teach others how much God loves them), that you will be given all the tools, learning, classes, people, and opportunities to reach that goal. My mission and purpose will be different than others. And that is the way it should be. But each of us has a something great that lies within. It's time to go find it!

Amy Oliver, LMT Health Coach relates her story (DestinedForFreedom.com/amy-oliver/):

I remember always feeling different . . . but didn't everybody? As a teenager I guess I simply went along with the assumption that everyone experiences feelings of "isn't there something more?" Don't we all ask the questions, "Who Am I, Why Am I Here, Where Am I Going?" It was only through experience that I began to realize not everyone thought the way I did, or pondered those all important questions. As I began to receive comments from my peers like "You're weird" (in response to my asking them "Don't you ever feel like there's something more?") my confusion, and determination to find out, deepened.

As I started 8th grade at a new school I felt all the awkwardness of a young girl gearing up to navigate the pending social situations. I was standing in line waiting for math class to open when a curious, blonde haired boy asked "Who are you?" I froze . . . the way he phrased the question paralyzed me for some reason. I just couldn't answer him! It wasn't that I didn't realize he was simply asking for my name. . . "Who are you?" was just way too deep for me to respond to in an instant—besides, I didn't know! He asked it a second time, and again I had the same reaction.

That has been one of my most memorable experiences and it marked a place on my journey with what I knew to be the most vital challenges I would face: To discover the answers to those questions! Along the way I've met others seeking the same, excited by the journey, but of course with responses as unique as they are.

At times I feel like Alice in Tim Burton's *Alice in Wonderland* as the Mad Hatter sets her down in frustration: "You're not the same as you were before. You were much more . . . muchier. You've lost your muchness!" The sense that I've had a "before" and that I am sent to fulfill a promise to live my "muchness" has been the driving force behind my continual seeking, finding, and shaping "Who I Am, Why I Am Here and Where I Am Going" I highly recommend the journey . . . wanna come?"

Martina Muir of www.MartinaMuir.com:

I cannot remember an exact moment that I knew I was supposed to help others in this world. Even at a young age, I remember yearning for a time when I could reach out and influence the world for good.

Oftentimes, while going through difficult challenges, I would think of ways to take the lessons I was learning at that moment and remember how it feels so later I could connect with others going through the same thing. It felt like I was mentally and emotionally "taking notes" and storing them up for a later date.

Occasionally, people would come into my life that needed to hear my lessons and experiences to help them deal with whatever they were going through. It fueled my soul as I watched their pain lifted after sharing things with them.

Then I started to notice that the desire to help more people started to drastically increase. It became a burning desire that would absolutely consume me if I didn't take action. This is where I am today, dedicated to serving and helping others who need what I have to offer. I have been lost in the dark, and I want to show them that there is light on the other side.

What about you? Did you have one defining moment? Or has there always been this knowing? If you haven't experienced either, I hope this book will inspire you to step forward and share your brilliance with the world. You CAN make a difference. You are important!

Phase 3: White

I sat down one evening to teach my six children the Parable of the Quartz. I asked them to tell me what they thought each phase symbolized. On "white," Joshua (then eighteen years old) said he thought of a white flag of surrender. Up until that point I had viewed "white" as purity. But Joshua's insights about surrender added a whole new depth to this phase of the process.

Truly, it is through surrendering to Christ that He is able to make us pure and clean. "Though your sins be as scarlet they shall be as white as snow. Though they be red like crimson, they shall be as white as wool" (Isaiah 1:18).

Surrender

In April of 2011, I was in Salt Lake City for Kirk Duncan's Present Yourself training. While there, my left arm seized up, and I couldn't lift it even halfway up without experiencing excruciating pain. Having broken my right humerus in a car wreck at seventeen and sustained radial nerve damage, I knew the familiar twinge of radial nerve problems. My friend Martina Muir was attending the training with me. She suggested that her husband, Jason, a personal trainer and owner of Firehouse Fitness, would be able to help me. So that night after class, I let Jason work on my arm.

He explained to me that emotions or stress had lodged in my shoulder muscles and had caused them to draw up into a knot. This knot obstructed the signals my nerve was trying to send down my arm to make it move. The nerve had to fire stronger voltage to communicate, hence the pain. Jason began kneading my arm in different places, starting at my armpit all the way down my arm. The pain was excruciating. In essence, he was breaking down the knots where my muscles had connected in ways they shouldn't.

I've had six babies all natural, and this was on par with that level of pain. I wasn't crying, yet tears were streaming down my face. Jason explained that "pain is weakness leaving the body." As he worked on each area, he would tell me, "Relax into the pain. Relax into the pain." As soon as I would relax, the pain would subside, and he could move to another area. He worked on my arm in several segments, giving me time to rest in between. I felt nauseated, which he explained was a good sign. It meant the nerves were communicating again. I broke into trembling chills like I'd had after childbirth. Again, he explained this was a good sign.

Finally, when he was done, I could lift my arm above my head without any pain. Sure, I was sore. I even had a few bruises from this Herculean body builder kneading my arm, but the difference was night and day. He then taught me stretches I could do and gave me a hard rubber ball I could lie on and massage the muscles in my shoulder, arm, and back.

He strongly advised me to work on releasing the root emotion behind the problem; otherwise, my problem would return.

I learned something incredibly important from Jason: the value of pain. I realized that in the past, I had avoided pain at all costs. I never would have guessed inflicting more pain on my arm would actually cure it. But Jason taught me that muscles are not supposed to hurt when you press on them. As long as the problem isn't caused by an injury, pressing on the muscles is a good thing. Pain is weakness leaving the body.

I also learned from Jason that the fastest way to eliminate pain is to relax into it — surrender to it. When we experience pain and trauma in our lives, the fastest way through it is to surrender to it. Allow it to be. When we tense up and fight, we only prolong the agony.

Victoria Fielding, author of *A Piece of Time* (www.LightSojourn.com), is the academic director of a residential treatment center for troubled teens. While a devout Christian herself, Victoria is unable to use "God" or "religion" to help these distressed youth. Their parents send them to this center specifically because they expect them to be treated without bringing God into the equation. Because of this, Victoria's heart yearns to share God's light with these youth in a way they can connect with. This is why she wrote her novel, *A Piece of Time* (which I highly recommend).

As Victoria works with these youth, she teaches them coping tools. The first of these is "Radical Acceptance" or what we might call "Surrender." Here's what Victoria has to share about this tool of Radical Acceptance:

> We may be paralyzed by an unrelenting sense of unworthiness. We may feel victimized; we may lapse into self-pity or depression in the face of what we encounter in life. Yes, it may be unfair—the victim of repeated abuse would say it IS unfair—WE would say it was unfair for her to endure what she did.
>
> But yet, it has happened, and there is no changing what has happened. IT IS WHAT IT IS. The stroke, the ulcers, the cankered angry souls come from the refusal to accept what is.

Surrender is simply accepting what is. Jesus modeled this in Gethsemane when he began to take upon himself the pains, sicknesses, sins and infirmities of all humanity.

> *And [Jesus] saith unto them [Peter, James and John], My soul is exceeding sorrowful unto death: tarry ye here, and watch. And he went forward a little, and fell on the ground, and prayed that, if it were possible, the hour might pass from him. And he said, Abba, Father, all things are possible unto thee; take away this cup from me: nevertheless not what I will, but what thou wilt.* (Mark 14:34–36)

The sooner we surrender our will to God's will, the sooner we can fulfill our missions and reach the other side. On the other side of Christ's intense pain and agony was ultimate joy, resurrection, the presence of His Father, and the glory of eternity.

Often the greatest joys are to be found on the other side of pain. I think of the births of my six children. On the other side of that excruciating pain was exquisite joy. Words cannot convey the love and joy that fills a mother's heart as she holds her newborn in her arms for the first time. I believe mothers, of all people, understand best what it means to find joy on the other side of pain.

Throughout the remainder of this chapter, I'd like to share with you some real life stories of people who have endured hardship, surrendered to God, and come out on the other side better for the experience. Not only that, they are extending themselves, reaching out to lift others.

Liz King Bradley, daughter of God, wife, mother, coach (www.LizKingBradley.com), shares her story:

> At the age of four I was molested by a close neighbor. He was the neighborhood grandpa, whom we all trusted, parents and kids alike. It was terrifying, puzzling and paralyzing. I misinterpreted the yucky I felt in the experience, and owned it as part of me. I heard all my life that I was a child of God, but now I felt ashamed that I was God's child, and I should be better. This lasted about 27 years. I spent the majority of my life trying to show that I was not yucky, while secretly believing that I was, that something in the core of me was fundamentally wrong.
>
> As a youth (12–18) I participated in a program of personal development designed to help me remember my divine nature and bring me closer

to God and reinforce His love for me. It worked. I still had a lot of mixed up beliefs, but now I at least had a hope of being divine instead of bad.

As a young mom the baggage really came out. I struggled with depression, split personalities, same sex attraction, rage, and anxiety. My primary reproductive organs developed a condition requiring their removal.

The process of letting go of my uterus and coping with the emotional traumas brought me continually to my knees. Having addicts in my family, I utilized the 12 Steps of Alcoholics Anonymous and that helped a lot. I was also inspired to use what I now know as energy work in clearing away the pain, bad connections, and disconnect from God. I came to know God and Jesus Christ intimately as I returned over and over again for the removal of pain from memories, guilt for wrongs perceived and real, and strength to get through the day without beating anyone. I have felt a warm blanket of light cover my life, and my soul. My whole being has been blessed with words of encouragement and love for others. I can often perceive things others cannot and have a faith that many don't comprehend. Through the pain I became lighter, clearer, and more able to help others recover from their own private fires.

Miko Batty (www.HigherVibrationalLiving.com) shares her experience:

Throughout my life I have felt I never fit in anywhere. I always had a smile on my face but deep inside I was miserable. I could not figure out what was wrong with me, I had a good life and it did not make sense to me.

As I grew into my teenage years I would pray every day that I could just die and leave all the pain behind. As I became a mother, my children were so dear to me and I loved them very much, but I did not feel worthy of them. I would look around at other people and say to myself, "They would be a better mother to my children than I am." I also would do the same with my husband. I did not feel worthy of this life I shared with my husband and children. I never thought that I would live to be my age. I was always sad inside and knew I would be taken any day. As the days turned in to years I began to question my existence. Instead of praying every day that my life would end I started to ask, "Why am I still here, what do I have to offer?" As I changed my thoughts and started to explore my options my world opened up to a whole new realm.

I was shown my purpose by Our Loving Heavenly Father. As I saw my life before me I started to understand that the feelings I was experiencing towards myself were not all my own. The feelings of unworthiness, undeserving, self hate, and other loathsome thoughts were passed down from generation to generation. It was time to clear up those negative thoughts.

I began working on myself to clear the self-sabotaging thoughts and actions through energy work. I was guided to many different energy modalities. As I started to clear the blocks within myself I saw the amazing transformation towards myself and my life. I was clearing old generational patterns that have been passed down many generations. As these clearings took place my world opened up to a new beginning.

I am so grateful for the experience I have gone through. I've made it my mission in life to help those who have negative feelings that hold them back from their true self. Finding my truth has made my life transform in all areas. I feel I deserve to have the best life can offer and I am worthy of it.

Throughout my clearing I have learned that so many people in today's society have similar negative thoughts about themselves and are attracting unpleasant circumstances into their lives. I am dedicated to teach others the way out of darkness and into the light of this marvelous existence.

Carolyn Murphy of www.familytreequest.com shares her journey:

When I was twenty, I married a man who was raised in an alcoholic home. In spite of our best intent for success, we began to learn how the heartbreak of dysfunction and stress in our family lines was affecting our experiences together. After the birth of four children and as our marriage disintegrated into divorce, I felt the devastation of the unraveling of our family unit, the blighted hopes of broken dreams and the agonizing distress of watching my children suffer emotionally in ways which were beyond mortal description. I saw and felt my own heart-wrenching states of anguish, distress, deep sorrow, and unbelief at "How could this be happening to me?" My emotions and the emotions of my children were misfiring in every direction, it seemed.

Sometimes I felt out of control. Always, I was being stretched to my limits. I knew the fire of adversity as if it were a constant companion—not yet experiencing its incredible refining and purifying power, but feeling its extraordinary pain—all the while assuming that lasting wounds and scarring would accompany this unwelcome guest. I traversed the path of unsettling self-doubt, gut-wrenching grief, shattered dreams and broken promises. I was able to combat the fear with faith and rise to the mountain peaks of hope on a trail I blazed in spite of the agony and with the help of God and friends along the way.

Because of the solutions and inner strength that arose out of deep difficulty, I have learned for myself that answers to life's perplexities are only a prayer and an inspired thought away. Out of the dark with one light-filled step at a time, I have gained the strength and the power within me that ignites and maintains my personal and family purpose. I have experienced the joy of seeing several of my children rise beyond their pain to become honorable and contributing husbands, wives, and citizens. I also gained deep feelings of empathy for those who have undergone family difficulties with all of the accompanying spiritual and emotional tentacles. I have compassion [for] those who enter marriage feeling like they are already wounded warriors and who desire to do their personal best, yet they don't know HOW to create a functional family since their homes of origin may have contained extreme stress, sorrow and dysfunction.

Fueled by my desire to bring the light of new hope to those who are struggling, I founded www.FamilyTreeQuest.com where individuals who desire to create positive change in their family and family lines can join a worldwide movement of people whom I call TODAY's ChangeMakers. At Family Tree Quest, ChangeMakers can begin to find time-tested, principle-centered solutions to helping each other, healing relationships and growing in spite of challenges. By sharing the light of our combined understanding and knowledge, we stand together to heal the heartbreak of dysfunction and stress in families while creating safe, secure and peaceful relationships at home. My inLIGHTened TODAY series is one way I will turn my pain into purpose. I'm happy to now share what I know about seeking, loving and embracing the light. I know, from experience, that light always awaits those who seek it, and a journey toward light is definitely a journey worth taking.

JoAnna Ashley of www.healing4bodies.com talks about her healing experience:

The most life altering and path changing point in my life came at the end of pain, and lots of it. At 20 years old I was officially diagnosed with fibromyalgia. However, taking into account the symptoms and health issues I had all my life, I had actually had it since I was at least 6. At this same time I was also dealing with debilitating arthritis in my hands, and infertility issues. I felt like all was lost and that I would just get to live a miserable life and eventually die.

I prayed to have relief or an ease of the symptoms, and sought out many methods to try and make life bearable. Nothing really was working and I just continued to get worse. Then came the light, but I didn't really want any part of it. My sister through another person introduced me to Energy Healing and Foot Zoning. I remember at the time I was introduced to it all I kept thinking "This is voodoo and witch craft. You can't do this." The reel that played in my head said that this wasn't ok. Being so desperate for improvement and healing though, I decided to try it. Imagine my surprise when it actually healed some of my symptoms! I continued with it and in two months my husband and I were pregnant for the first time. Within eight months the fibromyalgia and arthritis had been completely cured. More so than any of the physical healing though, was the emotional and spiritual healing I experienced from years of physical, mental and sexual abuse as a child.

I know without doubt that had I not been in so much pain and thought life so unbearable, I never would have entertained the use of Energy Healing. I realized in hind-sight that my fear of it being "voodoo" or "witchcraft" didn't stem from God's truth, but rather from misperceptions I had been taught. Once I experienced so much healing though, it opened doorway after doorway. I, in turn, have since studied Energy Healing, Foot Zoning and other alternative modalities in-depth and have seen my life and my family's lives transform before my eyes. I have been able to help some of my family find the healing in their life as well as my clients and the ripple effect has been so amazing to see.

My conviction now is that pain only exists as long as it is serving us. Once we have learned what it was teaching us, it can, and will quickly leave. Whether it be spiritual, emotional, mental or physical pain, I believe and know with all my heart that there is healing and wholeness waiting at the end of the lesson. I heard it summarized best this way: "Pain is God's way of letting you know you're off track." Since our spiritual connection isn't always so open or receptive to God, he needs another way to catch our attention so we would know where to heal within ourselves.

Lisa Rae Preston of www.StepIntoDestiny.com shares her story:

The first part of my life could be characterized and summed up in one word.
Broken.

Years of childhood abuse had shattered my body, soul, and spirit. My love for writing and desire to connect with God kept me sane as did my strong and safe grandmother. Her love and stability gave me a foundation on which to stand.

Thanks to the ability to separate myself from the memories of abuse, intellectually I lived life oblivious to the pain of the past. I completed college, got a master's degree in education, and taught elementary school. My class was known for fun, adventure, creativity and always doing something new. I enjoyed my life. Yet, I walked crippled and unbalanced and occasionally struggled with depression.

When my grandmother passed away, all that I had depended on to hold me up at the core vanished with one breath. I fell into a heap, curled into a fetal position, and sobbed . . . for months.

Utterly at the end of myself, with no self-created props left, I reached out to Jesus. His everlasting arms cradled me close to His heart and continued to hold me through the process of being reknit together by Him.

The journey through depression and brokenness took almost 5 years. I met face-to-face with the hideousness of my abuse, face-to-face with demonic spirits, face-to-face with a shattered life overflowing with shame and fear.

Gloriously, in the middle of every healing moment, the face of God met my own. His eyes gazed into mine with the purest passion, lasering away the shame. His words, whispered in my ear, taught me how precious I was to Him. His incomparable love washed over me, restoring my innocence.

God literally took all the pieces of who I was and put them together, in the most beautiful way, with exquisite tenderness and compassion.

Being knit back together hurt beyond heck. But the process of restoration brought treasures, jewels of strength, love and new vision. God showcased the beauty of the landscape of His heart. He looked into my eyes and allowed me to see the beauty of my own landscape—all the treasures He'd planted in my soul's garden.

I am convinced that we can never know the vastness of how precious we are until we look into the face of Jesus.

And do you know what? He's given me a new word to define my life. I laugh with joy as I type...

. . . Whole.

Yes! Not only did He bring me back together, He redefined my identity and revealed my mission and passion in life. Sharing the message of Restored Innocence.

Christ taught me how to access and draw all our talents into one place, from which we can be launched into our destiny with acceleration and an endless supply of fuel. He showed me how to connect with others at their core through the STEP into Destiny Core-Passion test. He revealed how He wants me to help others heal from their brokenness.

His deep desire is for intimacy with us, to draw us together into perfect Oneness with Himself. Whole and free! If there was one message I could share with the world, I'd shout it with the most exquisite of joys from the rooftops! "Look into the beauty of the landscape of His heart! Gaze into His eyes! You will not only see astonishing brilliance of the King, but He'll reflect back to you your own immense beauty. And you will dance into your destiny. Whole, restored, free to experience life with the innocence of a little child."

I believe Lisa Rae's story leads perfectly into the next phase: Clarity! Through the brokenness, the surrender, and the healing, Christ brings us to a place of clarity.

Phase 4: Clear

My friend Phillip Davis (TungstenBranding.com) is a whiz at naming and branding, and he helps business owners to gain clarity and focus. Over the years Phil has taught me volumes about clarity. When we're clear about who we are, where we're going, and why we're here, decisions are easier to make. We have a rudder to navigate our ship to its destination. But as long as we're unclear about these things, decisions take an inordinate amount of time, and we spend a great deal of our existence off course—simply because we don't know where we're going.

One exercise that Phil suggests is to state your goal and then ask yourself, "So I can do what?" For example, if my goal were to become a New York Times best-selling novelist, I would then ask myself, "So I can do what?" The first time I followed Phil's advice and used this technique, the results were surprising: somewhat depressing, yet eventually liberating.

Let me explain. I started by stating my goal "to become a New York Times best-selling novelist and earn $X per year in net revenue." Here's how it went from there:

So I can do what?
So I can influence millions of lives for good.

So I can do what?

So I can make a difference in the world.

So I can do what?

So I can hear my Father in Heaven one day tell me, "Well done, thou good and faithful servant."

So I can do what?

So I can feel my Heavenly Father's love and approval.

That was as deep as it went for me. I couldn't go any further.

Then Phil suggested that I turn it around and tie the goal to the final desire: "In order to feel my Heavenly Father's love and approval, I must become a New York Times best-selling novelist and earn $X per year."

Pretty silly, eh? In fact, it was so ridiculous, it was downright depressing to me. I'd spent a decade teaching women about God's love and grace through SheLovesGod.com, only to discover that deep down in the programming of my mind, I was still trying to earn my Heavenly Father's love and approval. It was driving my insatiable need to reach more and more people. It was driving my money goals as well because I've learned that people "vote" with their dollars for things that hold value for them. So if I was earning a certain amount per year, that would mean I was reaching the people who needed my message.

But I already HAD my Heavenly Father's love and approval. I knew that. So why was I jumping through these hoops to earn it? I was walking into my kitchen when suddenly it felt as if a heavy burden lifted from my shoulders. I realized, "I don't have to do all this stuff anymore!" The driving "have to" of it all was instantly gone, and I was left to ask myself whether I even cared to achieve these goals anymore. If so, why?

I came to realize that I do all these things to put positive messages into the world because I love my Heavenly Father and want to be a part of His plan. I love Him. He's done so much for me; I'd love to do what I can to help. This is a big shift from "needing" to influence millions of people because I'm trying to earn love and approval.

Interestingly enough, within two weeks of this revelation, I met Judy Rankin Hansen (TrustingSpiritNow.com), who began teaching me how to feel and experience my Heavenly Father's love and approval whenever I wanted. Through a guided meditation, I came into my Savior's presence and experienced God's love and approval in an experiential way. Judy went on to teach me how I could meditate and find that place when I needed it.

Had I not gotten clear about my heart's desire, would the answer have come? I doubt it. This is the power of clarity!

Ask Yourself This Question

One of the most powerful questions you can ask yourself is this one: "If you knew you were going to die tomorrow, and someone gave you a megaphone today to deliver any message to the entire world, what message would you deliver?"

The answer that comes first to your mind is often the most important thing to you. If you start delivering that message in everything you do—the way you live your life, the way you do your work, and the words you convey—amazing things start to happen.

Dolly Parton once said, "Discover who you are and do it on purpose." There's a lot of wisdom in that.

Visualizing Your Way to Clarity

In recent years, an increasing number of people have tapped into the power of visualization. What used to be considered "daydreaming" is now a viable method for accelerating toward your goals and aspirations. If you can't see yourself doing something, frankly, you won't do it. So now we have vision boards, and we use our imaginations to see and feel what it's going to be like when we achieve our dreams.

There is another power of visualization that I've found far surpasses this. It taps into a power far beyond our own. I first learned about it a few years ago when I met Judy Hansen. As I mentioned, the first guided meditation Judy led me on was to the Savior. It was so real that I felt as if I had actually visited with Him, felt His love for me, and given Him all my cares. It was so moving, there were tears streaming down my face. This particular meditation and a few that followed taught me that I could take these visual journeys myself. I could visit with the Savior in my heart, mind, and spirit. I could converse with Him like one person converses with another. Since that time, I've visited with Him many times.

Sometimes we have long, insightful conversations that tell me the direction I need to take next. Sometimes the insights are so powerful, I know I never could have discovered them on my own. Other times, when I'm very troubled, all I can manage to do is go sit with Him and put my head on His chest. After some time there, everything feels better. It's such an incredible peace simply sitting with Him.

Other times He takes me to different parts of the world or even to remote regions of the universe. We've walked on the beaches of Monterey, California; stood atop tall Irish cliffs; visited the desert; gone to Hawaii; and flown to the cradle of creation—a vast nebula at the center of the universe. Wherever He takes me, His creations illustrate His awesome power, majesty, and love. There is NOTHING that is too hard for Him, nothing that is too overwhelming. Not only have I found solace and forgiveness in handing Him my pride, my disappointments, and my mistakes; but I've also felt incredible joy in giving Him my hopes, dreams, and aspirations.

I don't claim to be a prophetess or to have literally seen my Savior face-to-face, but He does feel incredibly real to me. Whether you want to call it my wishful imagination, or a prayer, or a meditation, or my spirit communing with His, it yields wonderful benefits. I feel more joy, peace, clarity, inspiration, and love. He can drive away my darkest doubts, my greatest fears, and my severest worries. I don't know of any form of visualization that can top that!

How does it work?

I'll share with you a few tips that might help you train yourself to find this place where you can commune with Him. This is just my method. So feel free to adapt it until you find what works for you.

1) **Use a soundtrack.** I have a specific playlist on my MP3 player that I use to help me relax and find a calmer, more reflective state. I use a lot of Brian Crain piano music. (He's on iTunes.) I listen, breath deep, and relax.
2) **Start with a prayer and a very specific request.** The more specific I can be, the better. I might be looking for specific help in my business. I might be feeling overwhelmed and need clarity and peace. I might be concerned about one of my children. (Hint: You can take other people to Jesus in your mind! I've seen miracles happen with this.)
3) **Have a routine** for entering into the Lord's presence. After the prayer closes, I approach the Lord and enter into His presence in a specific way. It's just a "routine" that is personal to me. Find your own way of finding Him in your mind. It could be something like traveling across a bridge, passing through a curtain, or walking through a door.
4) **Once you've entered into His presence, ask Him your question,** or tell Him what you want to feel or know. Be still and listen to Him. He may ask you questions. Many times my sessions with the Savior are a lot like a "coaching visit" where He pulls the answers out of me.
5) **Devote the time.** I've spent one to four hours in this place. When I absolutely must go about my day, but the encounter has been so wonderful that I don't want to leave, I'll ask Him to come along with me throughout my day. I continue to walk and talk with Him in my mind as if He is right there beside me as I clean the house or work.

6) **Don't get frustrated** if sometimes you don't communicate as clearly. There are lots of times when the best I can do is find Him, put my head on His shoulder, and let Him hug me. Be there with Him and accept what comes.

So there you have my secret to visualizing. Spend a little time in the morning traveling to solar systems, nebulae, and the Milky Way with the Savior, and when you come back to your life, the goals you thought looked so insurmountable and overwhelming will seem possible.

Clarity, One of the World's Best Timesavers

In working with a lot of inspired creatives, I've noticed that one of the biggest time-wasters is indecision. We have trouble making decisions because we lack clarity about who we are and our overall purpose.

Clarity gives you direction. Direction enables you to make faster decisions. Faster decisions allow you to take advantage of the energy you have available and the excitement generated by your ideas. So let's say you have a storm of ideas raining down while you're in a flow state. When you have a clear direction for your life and business, you can quickly see which ideas fit and which ones don't. You can toss out the ones that don't fit and narrow your focus to the ones that do.

Let's say you've narrowed your choices down to three options that are in alignment with your purpose. Deciding which of those three to implement can depend upon the amount of available time, space, and resources.

For example, a gardener may choose from hundreds of seeds to plant. How does he know which ones to put in the ground? He looks at several things when making that decision:

- How much garden space do I have?
- How much time do I have in my growing season?
- How long does it take this seed to grow? Do I have enough time to grow it?
- Will this seed grow in my soil? Do I have the right kind of climate for it?
- Is the timing right? Is it the right season for the seed to grow?
- Will my family and I enjoy eating this fruit or vegetable?

If you have an idea, you can run it through a similar series of questions.

1) **Do I have space for this idea?** Do I have room in my life for it? For example, a decade ago, I knew I wanted to be a speaker, but I had small children at home then. Traveling wasn't a viable option. Now, as my children are older and my husband is home more, traveling and speaking are easier. I have the space for this idea.
2) **How much time do I have right now to invest** in this idea? If you're taking care of an ailing elderly

parent, now might not be the time for you to start a big, time-intensive project.

3) **How long will it take to get this idea to completion?** Do I have the kind of time available to wait for a harvest? For example, do you need the money immediately to pay your house payment? If so, an idea that could take a year to produce revenue shouldn't be your first choice.
4) **Do I have the right soil and climate for this idea?** Do I have the skill set, the energy, and the resources? Am I going to get bored with this idea? Do I have the money to hire the people who do have the skill set or temperament for the project?
5) **Is the timing right?** Let's say it's the heat of the summer and you want to grow broccoli. You probably won't have much luck since broccoli grows better in cooler weather. I've had many ideas over the years that I had to set aside until the timing was right.
6) **Will I enjoy implementing this idea?** Does it feel right? Is it going to make me happy?

So let's say you have an idea that doesn't meet one or more of the criteria above. You don't have to throw the idea away; you can just put it on the back burner to simmer a bit. Put it on your master list of ideas until the resources, time, and energy are available.

Give It Time

In my experience, clarity doesn't come all at once. It comes by degrees. For example over the last twenty-two years, I gained the understanding of who I am by degrees. For example, if I go back to the '90s, I progressed through these definitions of myself:

- I'm a computer trainer.
- I'm an entrepreneur.
- I'm a seeker of truth who builds other people up.
- I'm someone who loves inspiring others.

From 2000 to the present, I progressed through these definitions of myself:

- I'm a people collector.
- I highlight truth and talent.
- I'm a publisher of truth and a publicist of talent.
- I'm a Light Bearer.
- I'm a Tribal Leader of Light-Bearing Tribal Leaders.

We're always progressing, refining, and distilling our messages and who we are. Don't get frustrated if you don't feel like you have the "perfect focus" for your life, mission, and message. Clarity comes "line upon line, precept upon precept, here a little and there a little" (Isaiah 28:10). Be patient with yourself and trust the journey.

Phase 5: Transparent

After over a decade of writing regular articles on SheLovesGod.com, I learned that people respond and learn best from you when you're willing to be human. When you're willing to reveal your own flaws and weaknesses and what you've learned from them, people connect with you. If you're preachy with people, they close off. But if you reveal your own humanness and what you've learned along your journey, they can relate to you.

I remember writing in one book how my house was a wreck and a pedestal sink in my bathroom had been broken for a year before I finally had it fixed. My mom said, "I don't believe I'd tell that." But it's important to me that I not pretend to be perfect. I'm not. Over the years, I learned to be increasingly open, and I would have told you that I was transparent.

Then, something happened and I realized I wasn't as authentic as I thought in some areas. I became certified in SimplyHealed™ in October 2011, and I became acutely aware of the signals my body was sending me. It's almost as if our bodies are little babies without any way to verbally communicate with us, so they get our attention with an ache here, a pain there, a twitch there. And if we ignore its messages long enough, the body allows us to get sick to get our attention.

I've noticed that as I pay attention to my body and address the root issue, emotion, or concern, my body feels and operates better. Yet in December 2011, I had a bit of a health concern that got my attention. I kept asking my body what it was trying to tell me. The only thing that came up was this reoccurring feeling I had that I'm not making a big enough impact, that I'm not reaching enough people, that I'm not living up to my potential. "Mediocrity" is the word that kept coming to mind.

I asked myself how many people I'd have to influence to feel satisfied and used kinesiology to ascertain the number. You know what it was? Ten million! I was feeling I'd have to reach and/or influence ten million people to be satisfied with my life. Isn't that downright ridiculous?

Finally I turned to Karol Truman's book, *Feelings Buried Alive Never Die*. When I looked up the ailment associated with my symptoms, I found the root cause to be an injured ego or "unexpressed and unresolved hurts."

Going on these clues, I began asking myself in what way my ego had been injured and what hurts I had not expressed or resolved. I'd done so much work that I would have thought these things had been addressed already. But I decided to trust that there might still be something there. I took some time to ask prayerfully for guidance, and I listened.

Then the answer came. It was something deep within my past, all the way back in my childhood. You may have heard me talk about how great my dad was and how he built my confidence and trained me to share what I've learned. What I don't talk about much is that once I entered elementary school, things were quite different. People didn't strain to listen to my every word. My peers didn't think I was the best thing since the invention of color television. I had friends, but I was on the shy side. In fact, by the time I entered a new school in sixth grade where nobody knew me, I was the geeky teacher's pet that schoolmates ignored.

My middle school and high school years weren't much better. Most of the time I felt as if I was invisible. I got good grades and had a few good friends, but I'd hardly call myself popular. I didn't strive to be popular, either. I remember saying things in a group and nobody even acknowledging that I'd said a word. I didn't feel heard by or of interest to the vast majority of people.

As I reflected on this ego bruising from childhood, I realized something incredibly important about my motives to be heard today. I was trying to fill a childhood void. I was still trying to be heard, trying to prove that I have something of worth to say, straining to be myself and accepted by my peers.

The realization was sobering. I'd never considered myself someone who worried about being popular. I would have told you my motive in getting my message out was to change lives for the better, to help people, to make a positive impact. Surely it wasn't this sad pathetic motivation of a sixth grader in a new school, unable to fit in!

Yet, the more I faced the facts, the more I realized the truth. Sure, I had good motives, but mixed in among them was this "neediness" to be valued, appreciated, and to fit in.

Once I recognized these old programs running in the background of my mind, I set to work removing them and implementing new beliefs. I installed new beliefs like:

- I let go of the need to belong.
- I let go of the need to fit in.
- I let go of the need to be popular.
- I let go of the need to have large groups of people follow me, like me, or be my fans.
- I let go of the need to be validated by other people.
- I let go of the need to have ten million fans.
- I let go of the need to have any fans.
- I let go of the need to influence or be an agent of change for others.
- I let go of the need to prove anything to myself.
- I let go of the need to prove anything to the world.
- I let go of the need to prove anything to God.

That last one is a big one. But I believe it's in my highest good to let go of that need. Why am I trying to prove anything to God? He already knows who I am. There's no need to prove what you already are!

- I can be me, and people like me and are attracted to me.
- I am somebody.
- I matter.

- I offer value to the world.
- People want what I have to offer.
- Who I am is more than enough.
- I am content just as I am.
- I am content being a mother.
- I am exceptional.
- I am a daughter of God.
- I am amazing, unique, and beautiful.
- I am brilliant
- I am feminine and strong.
- I am determined and resilient.

Why had I been on this insatiable quest to prove something? Because I'd been trying to fill a void created in childhood! The thought did occur to me that if I installed these new beliefs, I might be a completely different person. Maybe I'd abandon writing, speaking, web designing, and Facebooking. Without the driving need, would I be someone else?

I decided that if I was, that would be okay, but I suspected that the underlying "neediness" was bleeding through. I believe that when we operate from neediness, we actually repel the things we're trying to achieve or acquire. Think of the overeager guy who chases after the girl. Think of the money that never seems to arrive when you're desperate to make ends meet. The needier we are, the more we drive away what we desire.

When we let go of our neediness and accept what comes, things start to flow.

A few weeks passed after this, and the shift that occurred was significant but not what I expected. I still wanted to write, I still posted to Facebook, but what I posted started to shift. I became bolder. I posted what I believed about liberty and political matters. I became more vocal about my faith and my beliefs. The strongly held beliefs and values I once tempered because I didn't want to offend anyone started coming out boldly and without reservation. I once told myself I didn't want to offend others who believed differently, but the truth is, I was afraid other people wouldn't like me if I shared what I really believed and felt strongly about. I might lose fans; I might get "unfriended." What if people didn't want to do business with me? That was the root of it.

So when I cleared away this neediness to be liked and have fans, what was left was the real me—a bold me. What I've found since then is people respect me more for standing by my convictions. Sure, I get responses from people who disagree, but I don't respond to them the way I used to. I don't feel the intense stress and anxiety that I used to. There's no fear anymore.

I stand by my convictions, but I respect others' opinions as well. I don't have to have the last word. I don't feel compelled to change their minds. They have every right to have different beliefs. That's okay. They aren't me. I'm the only Marnie Pehrson in the world, and I feel incredibly liberated to be the authentic me.

I feel what the psalmist said: "The Lord is on my side; I will not fear: what can man do unto me?" (Psalms 118:6) Or as Paul wrote the Romans, "For I am not ashamed of the gospel of Christ."

So, I ask you, is there an underlying need or void that drives you? What if you released it? It is an incredibly liberating experience to let it go! I feel like a new woman, free to be or do anything I choose!

The Painful Transition of Transparency

We'd just had our "Transparency" day at the 2009 Light the World event and had come back to start the final day. One of the ladies came up to me and told me she almost hadn't come back for the last day. She said day three (Transparency) had been so difficult for her that she didn't think she could keep going. She almost stayed in her cabin and blew off the last part of the retreat, but decided she needed to see this thing through.

No, we didn't give our participants anything particularly difficult to do on Day 3. But what Day 3 represented was this authenticity that many find extremely painful to face. Imagine yourself as a glowing ball of light with all the potential and greatness imaginable. You've suddenly gained clarity about the magnitude of who you are. You're exultant; you're excited. But then you realize that on this ball of light is a black blob. Even if you don't see it, other people can. At the very least they will sense that there is something incongruent about you. This affects who is or isn't attracted to you. If you're an entrepreneur, it affects your wallet because you are out of integrity and people sense it.

Once we've gained clarity about who we are and our relationship to God, we suddenly become aware of our flaws. Even if we can't put our fingers on exactly what it is, we know something is wrong. This is the point where many people give up. We think things like:

- Who am I to be teaching this?
- I have my own problems.
- Everyone's going to see I'm a fraud, an imposter.

Many times life will hand you an extremely difficult challenge at this point in the process, just to illuminate your weaknesses—just to show you how much you do NOT know. At this point, we're prone to lament, "My life is falling apart. What if everything I've been teaching people isn't true? I should throw in the towel."

For me, transparency showed up as a challenge in my marriage. Over the course of three very painful months, I came to realize that despite my quest to be authentic and put myself out there in a genuine way, there was one area where I was a complete and utter fraud.

Publicly I was transparent. I spoke my truth and walked the talk, but in my marriage, I didn't speak up for myself. I didn't express how I really felt. I was miserable. After twenty-six years of marriage, I was done. I was ready to walk away from it.

How did I get this far off track in the most important mortal relationship of my life? If there was behavior that was unacceptable to me, I sucked it up and kept my mouth shut. For twenty-six years I voted with my silence for things I didn't agree with. Then I hit a wall where enough was enough. For my husband, it seemed my dissatisfaction had come completely out of the blue. Why hadn't I said that I didn't like this or that before? Why hadn't I spoken up sooner?

After some reflection, I realized that it all went back to our first years of marriage. When we'd have an argument, he'd storm out, get in the car, and drive away, leaving me to wonder if he'd even come back. As a love-struck nineteen-year-old, I felt crushed. I seized up in a panic.

"What if he leaves me? I can't live without him." In order to protect myself, I made unconscious decisions in those fearful moments about who I would be in my marriage.

Suddenly, it wasn't safe to speak up. It wasn't safe to voice my opinions about money. It wasn't safe to rock the boat. And so I made an internal, subconscious decision to hold things in. Peace at any price became the rule. Over time, it affected our relationship, our children, and my health.

Interestingly enough, I believe much of my money-making ambition also came out of those early years. Most of our arguments were about how we would or wouldn't spend our money. I systematically created a safety net for myself so that if he did leave, I would be just fine financially.

So, during those three difficult months in the winter of 2010, I worked closely with a talented, empathetic friend who helped me work through the negative energy in my marriage. She helped me grow a spine, stand up for myself, and speak with the courage of a lioness. We consulted with our ecclesiastical leader, who encouraged us to be honest and let go of the fear of hurting each other in the process. By facing the dysfunctional communication patterns in our marriage, in time my husband and I were able to start working through our differences.

This was the transparency phase for me.

For one of my close friends, Leslie Householder (ThoughtsAlive.com), the transparency phase looked different. For years she'd been teaching people the laws of abundant living and helping people use those laws to obtain prosperity. Then, something happened that sent her finances into a tailspin, and she began to doubt not only herself, but also her message.

I'll let her tell it in her own words:

> Our world turned upside down about 5 years ago. Everything that had been going so well (you know, all those reasons I wrote Jackrabbit Factor and Hidden Treasures in the first place) suddenly imploded. Well, not suddenly: It actually all seemed to happen in slow motion—so slow that we hardly noticed what was happening.
>
> Let me back up. After our first big financial breakthrough in 2000, and after having enjoyed our new success for several years, we made some careless investment decisions. When we finally became completely conscious of the problem, we believed that we could "make" those bad decisions into good ones somehow just by "thinking right."
>
> A hard lesson I learned was that, sure, while it may be true that in every adversity there is a seed of equal or greater benefit, that doesn't mean the adversity will go away with right thinking. It only promises that something good can be born from it.
>
> It seemed that no matter how much positive thinking I mustered, our situation refused to

improve. It felt as though the principles were suspended on my behalf and it didn't matter how well I lived what I had been teaching, none of it seemed to be working as it had in the past.

So as you can imagine, one of my biggest stresses was figuring out what to do with the business. My husband had long since left his job to help me with it. But now, what about my books? What about our websites and programs? If the principles really didn't work anymore, how could I possibly continue teaching them?

I wondered if it was time to just pull all the books from the bookstores and issue a public apology. But, even as I fought my own demons, I continued to receive mail from readers all over the world who shared their success stories and profound gratitude for my work. Ben Southall attained the World's Best Job out of 34,000 applicants and credited my book for his success on a national news program. Publishers from other countries were asking for the rights to my book. Business owners were talking about how my programs had helped them multiply their revenues. Mothers shared stories of how they got the money they needed even after all appearances indicated it should have been impossible.

I read their expressions of gratitude and began to feel jealous of my readers' successes. I began to feel like a pawn—an instrument in God's hand, helping thousands of people achieve their dreams, but not being allowed to achieve MY dream, which was to just live a simple life enjoying my children and focusing 100% on my own little family.

Each time I seriously thought about quitting, I remembered those people and their stories. Simultaneously, I felt God telling me, "Keep teaching—you don't make the principles true or false by how well you live them."

Actually, we had quite a few arguments about that, God and I. But He always won. I'd throw my tantrum, and get bitter, rebellious and cynical. I'd try to ignore the needs of the business and just DECIDE to live the life I wanted. But then life always had a way of throwing me back into the work.

In my rebellious moments, I derived tremendous pleasure out of cleaning a toilet, or reorganizing a cupboard. After all, that's what normal people do, right? I just wanted to be normal. I wanted to let go of the pressure I felt to be a shining example of right thinking.

I can't tell you how many times I logged into Facebook, sorely tempted to update my status with what I was really feeling. I can be really good at sarcasm, but I also know how damaging it can be, so I resisted.

Over time, I began to learn new lessons. Deep, profound, clarifying insight into the same principles I had thought I understood before. My mind opened up and all the pain began to have purpose again. I began to write the *Jackrabbit Factor* sequel, *Portal to Genius*, to document what I was learning. We had new breakthroughs, and began to see our finances turning around. We had some of our best months we'd ever had, but still had a pretty deep hole to climb out of.

The final verdict was this: I knew the principles were true. I knew that things around me changed according to my thoughts and emotions. I knew that things went better when I lived with childlike faith, and took the time to "see" the outcome I really desired and answered the question: How would it really feel if . . .?

It's just that sometimes I didn't feel like doing it. I was tired. I was discouraged. I was impatient. I was embarrassed. Thinking right takes effort and intention, and frankly, sometimes it's just plain easier NOT to do it.

All of us go through this transparency phase, and it's not uncommon to go through it multiple times throughout our lives. In fact, the entire Light Bearer Cycle (aka Parable of the Quartz) repeats over our lifetime, continually refining us and making us shine brighter and clearer.

Phase 6: Refraction, Resonance, and Healing

You'll remember from the first chapter that quartz has three important properties:

- It refracts light.
- It maintains a consistent frequency (or resonance).
- It possesses healing and spiritual properties.

Let's take a look at each of these properties and how they relate to you as a Light Bearer.

Refraction

I occasionally visit a church building with a huge chandelier. The bottom of the chandelier is cone-shaped, and the top is a pillar that extends from the cone up into the ceiling, heavenward. The first time I visited this building, I loved the white light extending from the mass of crystal to fill the room. The second time I was there, I was able to sit close to the chandelier, a little bit under it. The more I looked up at it, the more I noticed all the colors coming from it (red, orange, yellow, green, blue, indigo, and violet), a million points of light emanating from the sea of crystal.

As I studied closely, I noticed that all of the light was coming from one main light source at the top that shone down into the center of the chandelier. As the light refracted through these thousands of prisms, it created stars of brilliant, colorful light. Then I noticed that the chandelier was positioned between two mirrors on opposing walls. This alignment created a sense of infinity. The reflection kept going on and on in a corridor of eternity.

I sat there for some time and pondered how similar we are to the prisms in this chandelier, especially when we combine our efforts. God and his angels can take our efforts and magnify them throughout eternity. They continue to reflect, and the things we do here influence eternity.

Each of us is different, and each of us reflects God's light in unique ways. In John 1:9, John says, "The true light shines through every man who comes into the world." Every man and woman who comes into the world has God's light shining through them. It's our choice whether we let this light continue to shine or whether we block it in some way.

I was telling a friend about my experience, and she exclaimed, "Oh, I volunteered one time in that building with some other women. Together we cleaned that chandelier." The chandelier was taken down, and the women sat around it on the floor, pulling out each individual prism, cleaning it, and reattaching it. This is done periodically because, if dust gets on the prisms, the chandelier won't have the same illuminating effect.

From this we see how important it is to keep our crystal clear so we can be a pure, clear conduit of God's light.

When we choose to join with others to magnify God's light, we magnify our influence. Our impact reverberates throughout eternity. If you thought you had to light the world by yourself as an individual prism, that would be daunting and overwhelming, wouldn't it? But if you join with others, you can create this amazing light source that leads heavenward, that extends through infinity, that affects eternity.

I did a search in the Bible for the term "light" and found an amazing passage in Isaiah. I know a lot of people are confused by Isaiah, but I'm an Isaiah buff. I think I like him because he foresaw our day. The following passage is extremely applicable to us. As you read it, think about the times in which we live and about how we can influence the world for good.

Arise, shine; for thy light is come, and the glory of the Lord is risen upon thee. For, behold, the darkness shall cover the earth, and gross darkness the people: but the Lord shall arise upon thee, and his glory shall be seen upon thee.

And the Gentiles shall come to thy light, and kings to the brightness of thy rising. Lift up thine eyes round about, and see: all they gather themselves together, they come to thee: thy sons shall come from far, and thy daughters shall be nursed at thy side. (Isaiah 60:1-4)

We are lights in a darkening world. The world in which we live continues to grow darker by the day. But against that backdrop of black is light. We are the light, and we shine even brighter against a midnight sky. We can make a difference, but we have to be pure, clean conduits. As we join together with other men and women who want to light the world, our influence for good will shift the planet.

Resonance

I found quartz's capacity to conduct a steady vibration very fascinating. Here's what I learned upon further study:

Every kind of piezoelectric crystal has a natural vibration frequency that is determined by its thickness. The thinner the crystal, the higher the frequency. When a crystal is made to vibrate at its natural frequency by the application of a voltage, the system is said to be in resonance. A crystal in resonance will maintain a constant, unfaltering frequency. When coupled with vacuum tubes or transistors, this constant frequency can be changed into a radio signal. Such was the design of the quartz radio, used primarily during World War II.

Another common use of quartz is in timekeeping. All clocks rely upon some form of oscillator to keep regular time; for example, mechanical clocks sometimes use a pendulum to regulate the motion of their hands. In a quartz timepiece, a small ring-shaped piece of crystal is made to vibrate at its natural frequency. A microchip reads how many times the quartz vibrates each second and uses that information to keep accurate time. Because the crystal's vibration is unfaltering, quartz clocks are among the most precise timekeeping devices, losing less than one hundred thousandth of a second each day. ("Quartz," E-Notes, www.enotes.com/quartz-reference/quartz. Emphasis added)

Notice that when quartz vibrates at its natural frequency (or is in resonance), it maintains a constant, unfaltering frequency. As a Light Bearer, I feel this is something that God has been trying to teach me over the last few years.

Many of us are surrounded by people living beneath their potential or who don't see our grand vision. Perhaps they're fighting against who we're becoming and what we want to accomplish. As Light Bearers we march to the beat of our own drummer, and thus we often deal with frequencies or vibrations that drag us down.

I've heard that crabs in a bucket will yank any crab making an escape back into the bucket. Just when a crab reaches the rim, up reaches a claw to drag him back down. How do you maintain a constant, unfaltering frequency in spite of what is happening around you? When there are crabs in the bucket clawing you back down, how do you keep on climbing? How do you keep on shining when mists of darkness clutch at you constantly?

This is my quest. I'm certainly not perfect at it, but I have learned some things that have helped me immensely. I'll share them with you over the next few chapters.

As a Man Thinketh...

Our thoughts affect our outcomes. It's easy to think negatively. It takes real work to think positively and look for the good when things seem to be going wrong around you. I've often said that the hardest work I've ever done is controlling my thoughts. Sometimes it's easier than others, but if I stay vigilant, the results are tangible.

The major shift in my business success came after I learned the laws of thought. I highly recommend reading Leslie Householder's various books and home study courses on the subject. It was Leslie's personal mentoring and years of striving to apply what she taught me that made the most significant shift in my financial and personal success in the last dozen years.

When you do find yourself thinking something negative, switch to something positive for about twenty seconds. You don't have to actually turn the negative thought around. You just need to think about something positive. You might think of something funny you saw in a movie or something cute your child said the day before. Or you might look at the blossoms on a tree and reflect on how beautiful they are. Take twenty seconds to switch to a positive thought, and you will undo the impact of the prior negative one and stop it cold in its tracks.

So let's dive into some more ways to maintain a constant, unfaltering frequency.

Forgive

This is a big one for me. I consider myself a forgiving person. I can let the occasional infraction roll off my back. I'm not easily offended. But when I must live with the constant ramifications of someone else's mistakes, that's immensely different.

There's someone in my life I've struggled to forgive, wrestled with my own bouts of criticism, condemnation, and frustration toward. It's not a pretty thing to know you have unkind feelings toward someone. It's not who I want to be. I want to be Christ-like, loving, and forgiving. Gritting my teeth and forcing myself to be that way doesn't quite seem like the same thing.

Jesus never seemed to be straining to forgive, never had to bite his lip and fight back a nasty comment. Those dark, ugly things weren't inside Him to begin with. It dawned on me that if I could see this other person through Christ's eyes, perhaps I could have those natural feelings of unconditional love and compassion. Maybe the irritation would melt away and be replaced with God's love.

One morning I woke early and decided to use the time in those peaceful, quiet hours to ask the Lord for the ability to see this person through His eyes. In my mind, He took me to a beautiful beach and had me take a seat on a log facing the crashing waves. He knelt in front of me, His hand on my shoulder, looking me in the eye. His were filled with infinite compassion and understanding.

He let me express the deepest desires of my heart—the type of person I long to be, free of these negative emotions, free to escape this cage I feel like I'm living in. It's as if there's this passionate ball of love and light that's crying to break free and express itself, but it keeps bumping up against negative limitations.

"If this person wasn't in my life," I heard myself telling Him, "I could be a good person."

I could see the twinkle in His eye and knew immediately how foolish that statement was. This person wasn't "making me have bad thoughts." The propensity to be critical, condemning, and judgmental was already there.

This person is in my life to give me a chance to overcome these feelings, to help me eliminate the black blobs that are stuck to my glowing ball of light.

"How do I get rid of this negativity? Please take these thoughts and feelings away from me," I pleaded. "Can I just give them to you? I would give away all my sins to know your thoughts, to be as loving as You are."

Again I asked to see this person through Christ's eyes. If there were some way to do that, perhaps all the resentment and bitterness would melt away.

At that moment, a situation from my past when I'd done something particularly bad came to mind. All the feelings of guilt and shame returned. It was a sin I'd already repented of, but the memory returned. After that event I'd felt despair and depression for quite some time. It was a dark time for me that I had no desire to revisit.

"That," Christ explained, "is how [this person] feels—all the time."

"Oh my. Really?" I remembered how immobilized I felt during that period of my life. I remembered feeling worthless, despondent, and as if there was no use trying to do anything. It was a horrible, debilitating feeling.

"You experienced this for a short season until you received My forgiveness. Imagine it stretching on for years. What might you have become?"

I then understood how and why this person had become so limited and responded to me negatively for so many years. In an instant, all that and more became clear.

And then Christ said, "Do you want to see how I see this person?"

"Yes, I do."

He showed me a beautiful young person, long before the mistakes had created a dark heavy cloud of guilt and shame. This shining, valiant individual with a future so bright and promising stood before me. And I began to weep. This was the beauty beneath all the rubble.

Instantly I felt my Savior's love for this person flowing through me, and I felt such an overwhelming need to apologize for being so blind for so long. I had belittled, condemned, judged, and criticized a fallen warrior, lying helpless, bleeding on the side of the road. I had not reached forth a loving hand. I had not dressed this person's wounds. I had not given this person a kind, comforting hug.

All I had seen was how this person's actions affected me. All I saw was how my life wasn't as ideal and beautiful as I wanted it to be—even needed it to be. I was too concerned with my rights, my needs, what I "deserved."

And then Christ's question came: "Will you help this person?"

"I will."

"You may not see results right away." He cautioned. "You may never see them at all."

"I understand."

"It's not about them changing. It's about you becoming."

"Yes, I understand, Lord. Where do I begin?"

"Why don't you just start with a hug?"

Gratitude: Look for the Good

Jesus taught, "Ask, and it shall be given you; seek, and ye shall find; knock, and it shall be opened unto you: For every one that asketh receiveth; and he that seeketh findeth; and to him that knocketh it shall be opened. Or what man is there of you, whom if his son ask bread, will he give him a stone? Or if he ask a fish, will he give him a serpent?" (Matthew 7:7-10)

God wants to give good things to His children, but nowhere does He say, "Gripe and ye shall receive" or "Whine and it shall be opened unto you." Nor does he say, "Pester me and you'll get what you want." He simply tells us to ask. Once we've asked and we've received an answer or a feeling of peace, we should expect that what we've asked for will arrive in God's good time. James 1:5-6 tells to "ask in faith, nothing wavering."

But sometimes we become discouraged, and we fall back into griping or doubting. It can be difficult to hold the right attitude — an attitude of faith and expectant hope — when circumstances appear as if you're standing still or even moving in reverse.

Several years ago, I performed a series of "experiments" (for lack of a better word) on the principle of gratitude. These tests were very enlightening and quite effective in not only shifting my attitude from doubt to faith, but also in unlocking the blessings that God has in store for me.

Whenever I would hit a problem or challenge, my initial human reaction was one of the following:

- Get angry, upset or pout.
- Start to lose faith that things are going to work out.
- Blame myself or others for my misfortune.
- Give up hope.
- Assume God is giving me a "serpent" when I asked for a "fish."

None of these reactions is productive or healthy. Each slackened my hope, weakened my faith, and distanced me from God and my goals. You see, all the promises are unto them that believe. None of these human reactions foster faith — none of them persuades one to believe. Without faith, nothing happens.

STEP 1: Decide what you want & when you want it.

Through these experiments, I learned to turn myself around when I caught myself reacting negatively to disappointment. Instead of entertaining myself with a pity party, I forced myself to examine the situation and ask, "What would have to happen in this situation to make me feel better about it? What do I want?"

For example, years back when my refrigerator and car broke down in the same week, I asked myself what would resolve the situation to my satisfaction. I wanted them both fixed and I wanted it done in a specific time and within a certain budget.

When a car I'd purchased with my savings blew a gasket three months later, I asked myself what solution would satisfy me. What I really wanted was to stop driving ten-year-old vehicles. I was spending more on repairs and replacing them than I would with a car payment on a newer vehicle. I wanted a van that was still under warranty, that ran well, and that I could rely on to take our six children where they needed to go. Instead of settling for what I could "get by on," I decided what mode of transportation would make me feel satisfied and secure.

STEP 2: Pray and get a confirmation that your desires are in harmony with God's will for you.

The next step is to pray about your desires and ask for a confirmation that what you want is what God wants for you. For example, in the case of the desire for a new van, I prayed for a few weeks about whether it was what God wanted for our family before the answer finally came—mere hours before the decision had to be made.

STEP 3: Write a gratitude statement and repeat it.

I am about to explain how I use a gratitude statement to shift my thinking. Please note that there is nothing magical or mystical about a gratitude statement other than that its ability to shift your mind from fear to faith, from doubt to belief. Remember that faith is the "substance of things hoped for and the evidence of things not seen" (Hebrews 11:1). Your ability to muster faith is critical if you want to take possession of blessings. Thus, a gratitude statement is simply a tool to help you achieve a level of faith that God can use to bring about your "miracle."

A gratitude statement should be written in the present tense and start with something like, "I am so happy and grateful now that . . ." It should end with a statement that ensures that everything happens in the best way. For example, I use, "I am so excited, thrilled, and amazed to see these things happening in ways that are for the highest good for us and all concerned. Thank you!"

Here's an example of a gratitude statement at work: Years back, because of some unexpected expenditures, I didn't have the money to meet some important obligations. My initial reaction was to get upset and begin to doubt. But then I remembered that the Lord has pulled us through in a pinch many times. He has confirmed to me time and again that He will care for us if we put our trust in Him. So, pulling myself up by my bootstraps, I took a break from my pity party and decided to use gratitude to change my attitude.

Instead of giving up hope and assuming the worst, I forced myself to take a hard look at my finances and make a list of what was due by a specific date. I totaled it up and decided on the dollar value that would satisfy my obligations and would meet our family's needs for a given period of time. In this case it was a three-day period. I decided on the dollar amount needed within three days to meet our obligations.

It was a rather large amount, and while my husband and I each had paychecks coming in over the next three days, they would only cover two-thirds of the amount needed. The rest would have to come from somewhere else. Instead of worrying about how this would happen, I crafted a gratitude statement, which I began to repeat to myself. It went something like this:

I am so happy and grateful that at least $X in funds are flowing into my bank accounts by [specific date], enabling us to meet all our needs and obligations for this period of time. I am excited, thrilled, and amazed to see this happening in ways that are for the highest good for us and all concerned. Thank you!

After offering a prayer of thanks that what I needed was on its way, I began repeating the statement in my mind and aloud. Remember, it's not God I was trying to convince—it was myself! The first day, when I was most discouraged, I repeated it nearly a hundred times. I'd say it out loud as I was driving down the road or in my mind as I was cleaning my house. It was amazing how quickly my negative attitude shifted to one of hope and positive expectation. I began to get excited about how the Lord would make that money flow into my bank accounts. I started each of the following days by repeating the gratitude statement whenever a discouraging doubt crept into my mind.

By the "deadline" I was still about 10 percent short of the amount specified, but in that time I'd been granted more time to meet certain obligations. In the end, I had what we needed when we needed it. The Lord provided.

I have used gratitude to activate blessings time and again and while my deadlines are not always met, my needs are. In the activation of blessings, you specify the what and let God take care of the when and how. It's an exercise in faith and patience, but it is amazing how gratitude can change your attitude and give you faith when you don't think you can muster another ounce of it.

So to recap, here are the steps for using gratitude to shift your attitude so that God can adjust your altitude:

- Decide what you want and when you want it.
- Pray and get confirmation that your desires are in harmony with God's will for you.
- Write a gratitude statement and repeat it as often as you can. The objective here is to bolster your faith and your belief.
- Continue to express gratitude to God even if things do not develop exactly when or how you specified.

As we cultivate a continual spirit of gratitude, we draw nearer to God from whom all blessings flow. Try the power of gratitude the next time life throws you a lemon and see if God won't help you turn it into some sweet lemonade.

You Are the Creator of Your Own Life

I grew up going to a small private Christian school. My entire sophomore class consisted of only fourteen students. Between home and school, you might say I grew up in a safe little bubble.

My mother took great care to make sure I had everything I needed, that my world ran as smoothly as possible. My father and I were close. He spent a lot of time with me, but because he wasn't into traveling, our family went on very few vacations.

My world was small, but I didn't know anything different. I applied for a scholarship to a university out west and got it. Amazingly enough, my mother let me get in a car with my best friend and drive cross-country from Daisy, Tennessee, to Provo, Utah.

It was one of the most carefree, fun times of my life. Here I was, out on my own. My mother wasn't there to select my clothes. My father wasn't there to make everything feel safe and secure. I had left behind the people who saw me only as the "shy, smart girl." I was free to reinvent myself and explore who I was for the first time.

Out west, I met people from different places. One of them was a young man from California named Greg. There was loads of chemistry, fun, and romance between us. Greg also had a familiar quality about him. As Dr. Linda Miles says, "The brain is looking for patterns." What I didn't realize at the time was that the "at home" feeling I had with this young man was a pattern that I had grown up with. That calming qi bubble feeling I had with my dad was also present in this relationship. I could be stressed or nervous, and Greg could calm me down instantly. No matter how scary the world seemed, with him, I felt everything would be all right.

We'd get in the car and drive to places I'd never been. We'd pack a picnic lunch, go to Deer Creek Reservoir, and sit for hours talking about the future—where we'd like to travel, what we'd like to do with our lives. It was fun and exciting, all with the familiar feeling of being "at home" with someone.

Greg was four years older than I was. He'd lived on his own in another country for a few years. He'd had several jobs and seemed older, wiser, and more independent. He didn't seem to rely on his parents and was quite independent for a twenty-two-year-old. He was fun to be with, and I believed he could show me the world. In the words of the old song, he was "someone to watch over me."

We fell in love. When we married, I had just turned nineteen, and he was a few months shy of twenty-three. At that point, the brief period I'd had to explore who I was and what I wanted from life ceased. Don't get me wrong. We were happy, but my life became about making my husband happy, about rearing our children, who seemed to come one right after another. Because I perceived Greg to be older and wiser, I deferred to him on decisions, much the way I had with my parents.

In 1990, Greg made a job transition that didn't work out. With him unemployed and me at home with two small children (ages two and three months), things were difficult. As a result of the financial strain, I started my business in May 1990. (You can read that story in Trust Your Heart: Transform Your Ideas into Income.)

For me, this set in motion a long line of years working hard to make ends meet. I did what I'd been trained to do in college: worked with computers. My husband found employment but ended up making half as much as he had before.

My business had to make up the difference. I did okay for a startup, but something was missing. Making money seemed so hard and required many long hours. My three oldest children remember me primarily as a quick-tempered mother who sat at the computer for hours on end.

I wasn't happy, but all I could do was work and try to fix the situation, to make sure my children had what they needed and that we had a roof over our heads.

I realize in retrospect that the relationship I ignored most over the years was the relationship with myself. I didn't know who I was, what made me happy, or who I wanted to be.

In the mid-'90s I took a DISC test that revealed that my natural abilities, and my adapted abilities were not the same. The test showed me to be a person who loved people by nature and would be happiest influencing them in inspiring ways. But I had adapted until my critical skills score (which was naturally my lowest) was off the charts. Why? Because I needed to make money, and computers were a way to do it!

I had sacrificed what would bring me the greatest joy for two things: money and what I perceived as security. Why? Because I had never taken the time to cultivate a relationship with myself. I didn't know who I was or what I wanted. Taking this test was my first real clue as to who I was and what would make my life blissful.

A Vow That Would Change My Life

At that point, I made an internal vow that, eventually, I would become the person who influenced people in an inspiring way—that I would work with my natural gifts and talents and find that place of joy. I didn't hop immediately out of my computer consulting and training business, but the transformation began subtly, slowly morphing into something much different.

In September 2009 I took a business trip to Utah and spent the last leg of the trip with my friend Judy Hansen in St. George. One afternoon we decided to visit Kayenta, a desert community that's designed in a very eco-friendly way. All of the houses blend in with nature so that you can hardly tell they are there. This artistic community features cactus, unusual vegetation, and a labyrinth to explore.

We took time to relax and enjoy this environment. I ambled thoughtfully through the labyrinth while Judy explored other areas. Then, while she was going through the labyrinth, I took a walk across the landscape, just investigating and taking my time to soak in everything.

The thought struck me on my walk that this was something I had never been allowed to do — or perhaps I had never allowed myself to do. My only nature escape had been walking across my own property, into the field and to the creek. I had never had the opportunity to spend all the time I wanted exploring any other location.

My husband, while he likes to travel, doesn't care to spend a great deal of time experiencing the locations we visit. For example, on our honeymoon we soaked up the scenery of California's Highway 1, driving to San Jose, San Louis Obispo, Santa Maria, and Monterey. We drove through nature but didn't get out, touch it, or let it become a part of us.

In 2000, on our fifteenth anniversary, Greg planned a second honeymoon up Highway 1. This time, I decided that if I was going to be there, I wanted to experience more. We were driving alongside the beach, and I told Greg, "Pull over. Let me out. I want to walk on the beach." I'd never walked barefoot on a sandy beach before!

Greg pulled the car over. I got out, rolled up my jeans, kicked off my shoes and socks, and started strolling along the beach. It was a chilly day, but I didn't care. I wanted to know what sand felt like squishing between my toes. I played on the beach, messed up the sand, and watched the waves roll in, wiping the beach clean once more. I picked up epiphanies and metaphors, something I love to do in nature. All the while, my husband stood there watching me, waiting for me to finish.

When we arrived at Big Sur, we got out at a park and walked toward the river. There was a wooden bench in the middle of Big Sur. I waded out and sat in the middle of the river with the water rushing around me. Such fun! Again, Greg stood on the side and watched.

In all our married years, these are the only two times I remember when we took any time to experience nature. Even then, I was experiencing and he was "watching over me." Other times when we've visited historic locations, my husband usually has everything scheduled so that we can stay on time with all the plans and hotel rooms he's booked from point A to point B.

It's great to have someone plan the details, but there's something about spontaneity that my soul craves. So in St. George in 2009, there I was with Judy, "Miss Fearless Spontaneity." There was no planning out days in advance. We never knew what we might choose to do or where we might go. We were flying by the seats of our pants. We were deciding on a whim to go climb a mountain in Zion National Park or take a trip to the desert.

We hiked to the top of peaks—something I'd never been able to do in all my life. I climbed to heights that would have sent my husband into vertigo. We meditated at the top of the mountain for hours. We took our time, soaking in every last piece of it, slowing down and finding the lessons in nature.

As I stood at the top of Canyon Overlook in Zion National Park, I felt completely and utterly free—as if someone had expanded my universe by a thousand. There was no rush, no hurry. No sense that someone wished I'd just finish up so we could move on to the next location.

It was as if someone said, "This bubble you've been living in isn't real. There's a great big universe out there with infinite possibilities." For forty-three years, I'd allowed myself to let what I thought others wanted or expected of me to rule my world. I'd let other people's comfort zones become the boundaries of my universe.

That was the turning point for me. I systematically started forcing myself to break through my boundaries of fear and embrace the life I want to experience. Thanks to this adventure, I've built an entire network of friendships with like-minded individuals who support and encourage me to be all that I can be.

As a result, my work doesn't feel like work. It feels like playing in a great big sandbox with all my friends. At home, I'm happier, too. I express more love and patience with my family. My younger three children have a mother much different from the one my older three did. They get a lot more of my time.

Take Time to Know Yourself

I highly recommend taking some kind of personality test to discover who you are at the core and what brings you the most joy. The things you are naturally good at are often the keys to finding your bliss. I love Lisa Rae Preston's Step Into Destiny test, which helps you uncover your core passion. You can take it for free at www.StepIntoDestiny.com.

I also recommend taking periodic vacations and making time for self-reflection—to step back and look at your life, relationships, and business from an aerial view. What's working? What isn't? Where do you see things going? Take an active versus passive role in creating your life.

Learn to Distinguish Your Desires from Other People's

Some people are very opinionated and know how they feel about everything. I'm not one of those people. If you're like me and more laid-back, sometimes our tendency is to defer to what other people want. Avoid doing this. If you want something, ask for it. Go for it. Back in 1985, on our honeymoon, I wanted to walk on the beach in San Jose. But my husband had already mentioned that beaches bored him, so I didn't even bother asking. Thus, I missed out on an experience that I really wanted to have.

Now, if my husband doesn't want to do something, that's okay. He doesn't have to, but that doesn't stop me from going out and doing what I want to do. If we're in a hotel in Orlando, and I want to walk by the lake and explore the Spanish Moss, I go down and do it by myself.

I've made a decision never to let life pass me by as I sit there in silence, afraid to either voice what I want or let go of timidity and take action.

Speak Up for Yourself—and Do It Soon!

I tend to be a peacemaker, and for years I told myself it was easier to "go along to get along." Honestly, I despise conflict. The problem with this tendency is that if you keep going along to get along, you usually end up somewhere that makes you miserable. You train others to treat you in ways you don't want to be treated. You vote with your silence for things that make you unhappy. And if you're like me, you'll blow a fuse one day when you've had all you can take. Then, everyone will wonder why you suddenly have a problem with how you've been treated for years.

Remember: You Are the Creator of Your Own Life

You may be in a marriage or part of a family, but you're also an individual with your own needs, desires, and interests. Remember that you are the creator of your own life, and you can choose how you want to live. Many times we think we can't create our lives, that other people won't like us making different choices. It's been my experience that all the things I thought my husband wanted me to do or not do were only in my imagination. He's been incredibly supportive of my interests and pursuits. He's never told me, "You're doing too much, you're flying too high. Don't do that without me."

It was I who thought the boundaries of his interests and pursuits were the boundaries to my world. The fact is, there are no limits to what I can create in my life. And there are no boundaries on what you can create in yours!

Trust your heart. Take the time to build a solid relationship with yourself. Follow your bliss, and "to thine own self be true." You'll be the authentic you, and there's something incredibly attractive about people who know who they are and who honor themselves and others.

Be Yourself and Let Others Be Themselves

Yes, we can impact others for good. Our influence and love can work wonders, but we MUST let go of the outcome. The only person we can really fix is ourselves. We have no right to impose our will on another.

Recently, I read Ayn Rand's *Atlas Shrugged* (Centennial Edition). Evidently, Rand journaled extensively about the characters, plot, and messages she wanted to convey before she ever began writing a novel. At the beginning of this edition, the editors included several excerpts from Rand's journal.

While I certainly don't agree with Rand's atheism, the woman was quite brilliant in many ways. I've learned an immense amount from *Atlas Shrugged*. One passage stood out to me. At first I was taken aback.

> It is proper for a creator to have an unlimited confidence in himself and his ability, to feel certain that he can get anything he wishes out of life, that he can accomplish anything he decides to accomplish, and that it's up to him to do it. . . .

> [But] here is what he must keep clearly in mind: it is true that a creator can accomplish anything he wishes—if he functions according to the nature of man, the universe and his own proper morality, that is, if he does not place his wish primarily within others and does not attempt or desire anything that is of a collective nature, anything that concerns others primarily or requires primarily the exercise of the will of others. (This would be an immoral desire or attempt, contrary to his nature as a creator.) If he attempts that, he is out of a creator's province and in that of the collectivist and the second-hander.
> Therefore he must never feel confident that he can do anything whatever to, by or through others. (He can't—and he shouldn't even wish to try it—and the mere attempt is improper.)

What? But what about the power of synergy? Synergy may be one of the most central themes of my life, and thus I initially recoiled at her theory. Yet, as I continued reading, I began to better understand her reasoning and found myself agreeing:

> He must not think that he can . . . somehow transfer his energy and his intelligence to them and make them fit for his purposes in that way. He must face other men as they are, recognizing them as essentially independent entities, by nature, and beyond his primary influence; [he must] deal with them only on his own, independent terms, deal with such as he judges can fit his

> purpose or live up to his standards (by themselves and of their own will, independently of him) and expect nothing from others. . . .

I've known many creatives (including myself) who were married to people of the opposite personality type, people not the least bit interested in their spouses' ideas and unable to fully grasp the logic behind their dreams. In fact, a friend wrote me within twelve hours after I read the above passage to say that she'd finally given up on getting her husband to support her in her mission. She felt she'd put her own dreams on hold waiting for him to catch up for far too long.

Her husband does love her and support her monetarily, but he's not ecstatic about her ideas and doesn't really "get" where she's coming from. He doesn't oppose her, but he's not interested, either. I think it's important to look at our definitions of support. Does someone have to "get" you to be a support to you?

My own husband has only read one of my twenty-two books, and that was a historical fiction novel. He doesn't get excited about my ideas. He doesn't get the core of what drives my passions. For a long time, I found this very frustrating. How could he even know me (or truly love me) if he doesn't get excited about my core passion in life?

But then I began to understand what Ayn Rand describes in that last paragraph: If we wish to be free to be ourselves, we must respect other people's freedom to be themselves.

If I waited for my husband to get excited about my projects, read all my books, or advocate for my cause, I'd never do anything. You are responsible for your own life and your own message. Other people are responsible for theirs.

You can be with a spouse who doesn't get excited about what excites you. I came to understand that the limitation was only in my mind. You are free to be you. You don't need a specific person to get you. God will bring people to you (and is bringing people to you) who do get you. When I let go of expecting my husband to be who I wanted him to be, I was able to see the many ways he does support me. For one thing, he never complains about me spreading my wings and doing my own thing.

Bottom line, I'm learning that if I want the freedom to be me, then I must allow others the freedom to be themselves — even if, in my view, they use their freedom to choose bondage.

James B. Moore of WebsitesThatInspire.com shared this story that is relevant to our discussion:

> It was my son's fourth birthday. We had a small family party for him, complete with cake and candles. We turned off the lights and lit the candles. As you can imagine his eyes lit up with childish awe when he saw his glowing cake coming toward him, while all of us sang happy birthday to him. Before this his older sister and brother had been sharing with him how if he made a wish and then blew out all of his candles it would come true, so he was really looking forward to

that moment. Then it happened, as I set the cake on the table in front of him, his older brother, who tends to get a little over excited at times, exhaled and accidentally blew out the birthday candles. The birthday boy's dreams were momentarily dashed, and this simple unintentional act caused sadness and disappointment for him. Luckily in this case we were able to re-light the candles quickly and he was able to blow out his candles in celebration of this moment in his young life.

From this simple and somewhat comical family experience, I learned a valuable lesson. All too often, in our attempt to be ourselves or in our attempt to run from ourselves and who we are, we end up spending all our time and energy running around blowing out everyone else's birthday candles, which unintentionally keeps them from being their true selves. In fact, I have worked in some corporations over the years where everyone was so busy running around trying to blow out each others' candles that nothing productive ever got done. It was not a fun or uplifting place to work.

I think it is very important as we begin to share our light and message that we first work to find out and become happy with who we are and learn to celebrate it. When we are clear about ourselves, we are better able to add to others' celebrations and not accidentally blow out their candles in our excitement to share ours. (Excerpt from A Pattern of Happiness audio CD, track 3)

Exercise Regularly

We only get one body in this lifetime. Unfortunately, I ignored mine for many years. I was too busy to give it the time and attention it needed. Frankly, I never enjoyed exercise, either. After twenty years behind the monitor, I had the "computer spread" and constant back and shoulder discomfort.

It wasn't until I was coming back from a Florida vacation with my family in August 2011 that I got a clear picture of who I wanted to be in two years' time. I envisioned the relationships I wanted, the kind of person I wanted to be, and what I wanted to do with my life.

As I did this, I realized that I didn't have the energy to be the person I envisioned. I also wasn't the high-energy, passionate person that I would need to be to attract those types of people into my life. Bottom line, something had to change. I needed to start taking care of my body.

So I came home and started taking vitamins and added walking to my daily routine. I did that for a few weeks, and then I started going to the gym a couple days a week. Over the next few months, I gradually worked up to going to the gym four or five days per week.

I've lost twenty pounds, I feel fifteen years younger—and, what's more, it's changed my outlook on life. I've found it much easier to cast out the negativity and control my thoughts when I'm working out.

In his A2B blog, Daryl O'Bryant wrote, "It requires almost no effort to see all that is wrong in the world."

Before I started working out, I was extremely good at seeing what was wrong in the world. I had to fight a periodic battle with negativity. As long as I'm in the flow state of my creative cycle, I'm fine. It's easy to think positively when I'm engrossed in a project. But let me cycle back to a rest phase when I've lost my zeal, and I have a tendency to sink into negativity and start griping about my life and everything that is wrong in it.

I've found that I have a much better attitude (aka control over my thoughts) when I exercise regularly. If I miss exercising for a few days, my thoughts invariably get more negative.

Is this because there is a mind-body correlation (master the body, master the mind) or is it that endorphins released during exercise just make life seem rosier? I posed this question to Daryl O'Bryant (our cross country Light Bearer www.Sub4Minds.com). Here are his insights:

> I believe that it is a combination of things. I believe that the mind-body correlation and endorphins are both components. I also believe that breathing in higher doses of oxygen is a big part. (The word "inspire" literally means to breathe, to draw air in.) More oxygen hitting the brain. More toxins being purged as you exhale more deeply and frequently.
>
> Movement is life! There is just something about it.

In its simplest form, it brings joy. We naturally understood this as children on the playground. Without really thinking about it, we remember it when we exercise, dance, laugh, etc. Oddly, joy brings movement. For example, when you receive some fantastic news, your body just has to jump up and down!

The mind, body, and spirit are all designed to move. To be in motion. To act. Especially when moving with direction and purpose, using our unique set of gifts and talents. This is the highest and best use of our mind, body, and spirit.

All of these things can naturally lift and brighten our outlook. But all of these things require a choice and effort. (And that is a whole other chapter!!)

In the end, I believe we choose how and what we see. We choose how and what we do. Perhaps another way to look at it is that we choose and create the environment that we live in. We choose and create our lives.

Use Music to Lift Your Spirits

I love music. It's been a critical part of my life from a young age. My mother made sure that it filled our home, and I started piano lessons at five. I love music. It expresses the deepest feelings of my heart. When I'm feeling down, depressed, or apathetic, the right song can lift my spirits and have me floating on air before I know it.

After a full, tedious day on the launch of my recent book, *Trust Your Heart: Building Relationships That Build*

Your Business, I was exhausted. I'd skipped my morning workout because I had too much work to do. My head was aching and I was exhausted. Yet I had a deep sense of satisfaction after my colleagues and I were able to take the book to #1 in three Amazon categories, including #1 Amazon Mover and Shaker.

I knew I should be celebrating, not feeling like I'd been run over by a truck. So I put on a song with a great beat, got up from my office chair, and started dancing. I danced all around, letting the music lift my spirits. By the time the song ended, my headache had disappeared. I kept dancing for thirty minutes or more, even roping in one of my colleagues to dance along with me virtually on Facebook. By the time our dance session ended, I felt fantastic, renewed, and energized.

That is the power of music AND the power of movement.

I hope these ideas for maintaining a positive frequency have been helpful for you. There are others I could add, like serving others, exploring nature, and incorporating things you love into your daily routine.

Most of all, look to Christ in every thought, in every circumstance. Read Matthew 14:22-33 about Jesus walking on the water and Peter taking a few steps on the water. There are great lessons here. The men were scared that Jesus was a ghost. Sometimes the things that look the very worst coming toward us are for our greatest good. When Peter kept His eyes on Christ, he could walk on water. When he became fearful and distracted by the winds and the waves, he began to sink. Keep your eyes on the Master.

Know that with the Savior's help you can maintain a positive frequency, no matter what is happening around you.

I love that quartz is used in radios. It's broadcasting its message out to the world—just as you will do when you learn to maintain a constant, unfaltering frequency.

You Are a Healer

My job is getting positive messages out in the world. With this task comes the question: How does one cut through the noise and information overload most people feel? People are constantly being bombarded with commercials, television, the internet, text messages, cell phone calls, and social media.

My colleagues and I are seeing a trend where people are starting to shut down. They have too many choices, too many options, and it creates immobilization. People stand still when they're overwhelmed and immobilized—even when a perfect solution is staring them in the face. So how do you get people who need what you have to offer to pay attention to you? How do you get them to come for your message, product, or service?

It can seem daunting and overwhelming to get one's message through this cacophony of noise. I've spent years pondering the question. The answer came to me as an epiphany.

I had been working long hours on my computer for several days. I was feeling overwhelmed, frustrated, and ready for a break. So I decided to go for a walk in nature. I was looking at the beautiful day—the blue skies, fluffy clouds, and gentle breeze on my face. The more I walked around, the more grateful I felt for our property, for the beauty of nature. The more grateful I felt, the more love I felt for my Creator for giving me the rich blessings found so freely in nature.

As my heart was drawn out in love, I felt my Creator's immense love for me and realized that God is constantly sending us a message through nature:

- I love you!
- Come to Me!
- I can heal you!

The more I walked in nature, the more I felt that love, and my soul was healed. I no longer felt overwhelmed or frustrated. I felt whole and loved.

I believe God has lots of messages and mysteries to share with us, but He doesn't throw all of them at us at once. He starts with a simple, clear call like the one above.

In every religion, creed, or belief, this message comes through loud and clear. It's the basic, simple message that permeates everything, carried on waves of light and on the breeze. I know you've heard it! I know you've felt it!

How can you and I get a message through to people like that? I believe we do it in the same way. Our message needs to be that powerful, that succinct, and that pervasive.

I began to think of my own message and how I could model the message of the Creator of the universe. I decided mine was, "I love you! You have an amazing message to share! Let's get it out there!"

I could go into the details of how that's done with article marketing, social media, writing books, etc. But that's just overwhelming to someone who is in pain and hurting, someone who has a message inside that feels bottled up. The message they want to hear is:

- I love you!
- You have an amazing message to share!
- Let's get it out there!

If you were someone with a message to share, that is all you would need to hear, know, and feel in order to come for help.

What about you? What is your message? What can you deliver in everything you do? What message can you emit to everyone in everything you do and say? It should have the same elements:

I care about you. You are of value.

Your clients and customers need to know that you care. Ask yourself:

- Who do you like to work with?
- What types of people get you excited?

Come to me

People need to know how to find you! Never has it been easier to deliver a message to the world with the advent of the internet, websites, social media, and video.

Don't be timid. Spread your message in every way you can so that people can find you!

How can you heal them?

God knows that people are lonely, sad, afraid, sick, and broken. His message is "I love you. Come to me. I can heal you!" This is the same message you're sharing as a Light Bearer. You have a solution (or medicine) to heal the world's malady. You have the keys to unlock its prison.

As a Light Bearer, you are a healer. You are a conduit and a reflection of the greatest Healer of all. Don't be timid about this. Embrace it. Think specifically about what you offer the world and whom you serve. How does your message heal people's pain and relieve their sorrow?

As you start with the love for those you serve and reach out in healing ways, people will be drawn to you. This should be the philosophy behind your marketing. The practical aspects involve articulating and systemizing your message in a way that can be conveyed to the masses—whether that's through books, ebooks, online courses, live training, webinars, teleclasses, DVDs, CDs, videos, etc.

BUILDING YOUR TRIBE

After making my chart of twenty people who've influenced my life and coming up with my definition of Light Bearers, I sat with this discovery for a week or so, just letting it marinate. As I did so, a question arose: "Now what? What do I do with this message?" I was so determined to find an answer that I devoted a Saturday morning to finding it. I went upstairs to a spare bedroom and opened my scriptures, offered prayers, and asked God to tell me what He wanted me to do with this new insight. How should I apply it practically in my life? I determined that I would stay put until I found the answer.

I began to meditate and envision myself having a conversation with the Lord. I got a few insights, but not any clear "marching orders" — which was what I really wanted. Determined to wait and listen for the answers, I stayed there for four hours. Meditating, dozing, pondering. Finally, in a flash, this image entered my mind. It was like watching a movie or memory in my head.

The Savior appeared in my living room carrying a large folded game board in his hand. He headed toward my dining room. Where my square dining room table normally is, there was a big round table. He set the game board down on the table, and it began unfolding rapidly until it covered the entire table. He motioned for me to sit down. I did, and He handed me a card.

It read, DRIVE TO KENTUCKY AND HELP YOUR FRIEND WITH HER BUSINESS FOR A WEEK. EARN $X IN GOOGLE REVENUES.

I knew what this card was referring to. Over a year ago I had taken a week to help a friend and ended up having one of my highest-grossing months ever in Google revenues.

The next card read, HELP ANOTHER FRIEND SELL FOUR OF HER PRODUCTS. EARN $1,000.

I looked around, and seated at the table were my twenty pivotal friends and family members. They, too, were getting cards. In the center of the table was a globe like the earth. As they sent something good into the world, they earned "Light the World Watts." The globe would get a little brighter. Then someone else would take a turn by helping someone at the table or putting something positive into the world, thus earning Light the World Watts. Each time this happened, the earth grew a little brighter. When someone needed something, it just came — whether it was money, time, or resources.

I soon discovered that the object of the game was to help the other players at the table in any way possible. By helping the others, we helped light the world. Lighting the world helped prepare it for Christ's coming.

So let's say we need money, or time, or resources, or energy to accomplish our objective (to light the world). Those things will come to us until we reach a saturation level where there is enough light to coexist with our Creator. In order for us to abide Christ's presence when He comes to Earth, there must be a certain level of light and truth among us. John says, "When he shall appear we shall be like him" (1 John 3:2).

Now, the whole planet is not going to achieve this all at once, but if we have a high enough number of Light Bearers, it is possible.

The beauty of the round table is that, as Light Bearers, we aren't competing with each other; we are working synergistically to bring light to the world. I realized that while Leslie Householder or Carolyn Cooper might be sitting at my table, they each had their own tables adjacent to mine. Together, everyone at the table represented twenty other interconnected circles. As we each worked to light up our own tables (our own circle of influence), our combined efforts lit up the planet.

It is through synergy that we transform the planet and prepare it for a millennial day. In 2000, I found this prophetic quote by Joseph Smith: "Christians should cease wrangling and contending with each other, and cultivate the principles of union and friendship in their midst; and they will do it before the millennium can be ushered in and Christ take possession of His kingdom."

When I read this, it resonated with me so strongly that I knew, just knew, that this was why I was on this planet—to help fulfill this prophecy.

And I believe this is done by working together to light the world. You do this by:

- Helping the other people at your table.
- Putting good things out into the world.

As you do this, as your focus is set upon building God's kingdom, the things you need will come to you.

Be a Tribal Leader

As a Light Bearer, you are either a leader of a "tribe" or a participant in that tribe. But what is a tribe? Here are a couple definitions:

"When your relationships with one person or more in a given niche reach the point that you deeply care about these people, and they about you, you are part of a new tribe." (Oliver DeMille, *FreedomShift: 3 Choices to Reclaim America's Destiny*, Kindle Location 2105)

"A tribe is a group of people connected to one another, connected to a leader and connected to an idea . . . A group needs only two things to be a tribe: a shared interest and a way to communicate . . . You can't have a tribe without a leader — and you can't be a leader without a tribe." (Seth Godin, *Tribes: We Need You to Lead Us*, Kindle page 57)

3 Roles of Light Bearers

Your "round table" is the start of your tribe. It's the people you trust the most, your inner circle. For example, Jesus had his closest allies (Peter, James, and John), all of whom were also his apostles. He also had hundreds of disciples and thousands of others who listened to His teachings. Some followed Him because they believed in His vision. Others were there for the "goodies" He could provide (healing, food, perhaps even entertainment).

You'll notice that His apostles got most of His time. He traveled with them and taught them. He also spent time with His disciples, such as Lazarus, Mary, and Martha. You'll notice that those He trusted and connected with most got the best He had to offer — the deepest insights, the most direct answers. You'll also notice that those who were closest to Jesus sacrificed the most and were the most devoted. They were the ones who stepped out of their safety nets and followed Him.

Jesus told the rich young man, *"If thou wilt be perfect, go and sell that thou hast, and give to the poor, and thou shalt have treasure in heaven: and come and follow me.' But when the young man heard that saying, he went away sorrowful: for he had great possessions"* (Matthew 19:21-22).

This story indicates the level of commitment Christ required of those closest to Him. Now, you as a tribal leader aren't going to ask people to sell everything they have and follow you. But those who are willing to commit more time, effort, energy, and resources to the cause will be the ones you'll most likely bring into your inner circle. It's the people who sit at your round table and work with you that you will entrust with the most confidence and the most insights.

There will be other people (like the multitudes) who follow you and your message, who advocate for your cause, who are a part of your movement.

Over the years, I've noticed that Light Bearers fall into three primary roles. These roles can also comprise your tribe.

1) **Thought Leaders** (aka tribal leaders) are people with a new system or method for sharing truth and freedom with the world. Ann Webb is a thought leader on LifeVision. Leslie Householder is a thought leader on financial freedom. Thought leaders are liberating captives with a new or innovative idea or method. Their core message is freedom; whether they realize it or not, they are lighting the way to financial, personal or political freedom. They may be liberating people from their past or freeing them to create their own lives. They are showing people to the tree—the love of God, or ultimate freedom.

2) **Advocates** tend to surround thought leaders. These people may follow several thought leaders. They are learning sponges, gathering in light and truth. They may eventually become thought leaders themselves, but for many it's not about the new idea; it's about applying the idea in a practical way. Advocates usually blend their own life experience, knowledge, training, and interests with the thought leaders' ideas to apply them in a unique way.

For example, let's say a woman becomes a Certified LifeVision Coach, and she's drawn to work with women (like herself) who've come out of abusive marriages. She can uniquely apply Ann Webb's material to assist a narrow niche of women who may never have found Ann's material any other way.

If you're an advocate, don't worry that you don't have a compelling "new" idea. Take the training you've received from thought leaders, combine it with your own life experiences, and start reaching out to the people with whom you resonate.

If you're a thought Leader, you need advocates because there's simply not enough of you to go around. The world needs your idea, and advocates are an ideal way to reach people in ways you never could on your own. The advocate acts as a bridge to your material. Women coming out of abused marriages may never think to look for LifeVision information, but they are more likely to be drawn to the advocate because the advocate knows their pain. To truly leverage your message, you need to have systems in place to create and foster advocates.

3) **Lamp Bearers** are in the trenches lighting the way for their families, friends, and neighbors. They may have no desire to own a business, teach a class, or mentor others. Yet they are affected by the message, perhaps indirectly by the advocates. They've found the light, and now they're sharing it in a natural, grassroots way. Lamp bearers embody the idea in their daily interactions. You've met these people. They have a glow about them. They're good people, serving and lifting others with their presence. A lamp bearer lives the light!

Lamp Bearers

I believe every disciple of Christ is a lamp bearer. Just as Jesus said:

> Ye are the light of the world. A city that is set on an hill cannot be hid. Neither do men light a candle, and put it under a bushel, but on a candlestick; and it giveth light unto all that are in the house.
>
> Let your light so shine before men, that they may see your good works, and glorify your Father which is in heaven. (Matthew 5:14-16)

Whether we're thought leaders, advocates, or people who care nothing about building a business or delivering a message to the world at large, all of us fill the role of lamp bearer. It's the foundation of who we are as disciples of Christ.

As a Lamp Bearer, you are so important in lighting the world. You are reaching family members, friends, and neighbors who might never listen to the thought leaders or advocates.

I think of people I've known throughout my life. One is my dear friend, Luanna Rodham (LuannaRodham.com). Luanna is a virtual assistant.

She hasn't written a book or created a huge online presence. She helps entrepreneurial women get their work done so they have more time to spend with their families. And that is Luanna's message: "Love your family." She conveys it without having written a single article on the subject.

It's what she models, and it's who she is. I've watched Luanna go through very difficult times. Several years back I observed her as she endured breast cancer, radical surgery, months of chemo, and finally radiation.

Throughout it all, she maintained her faith and praised the Lord and the miraculous power of prayer. What's more, she maintained her cheerful disposition. Watching one of my best friends go through this with such grace was one of the most faith-promoting experiences of my life. I've learned from dozens of experts and mentors throughout my life, but nothing has had such a visceral impact on my faith as watching my friend lean on the Lord in her darkest hour. I watched Him carry her in His arms and surround her family in what Luanna refers to as a "prayer bubble" that kept them at peace.

Recently, I've watched an older woman in my church endure something similar. For her, it's brain cancer, surgery, and radiation. Whenever she's given the opportunity to stand up and share her testimony, her smile is contagious. Christ's light shines in her eyes as she praises the Lord and speaks of the immense blessings that have come to her throughout this challenge. As she walks back from the podium, people extend their hands, clasping her fingertips as she expresses sweet words of encouragement and love.

But you don't have to endure something as dire as cancer to be a lamp bearer. I think of the young mother who attends every Sunday, sitting by herself with her small children. Her husband, who used to be faithful, now will have nothing to do with God. The burden of rearing her children to love the Lord falls squarely on her shoulders, and she rises to the occasion with strength and grace. Sure, she has her moments when she feels overwhelmed and the tears come. But through faith in the Lord Jesus Christ, she endures and is strengthened to bear her burden.

I think of another woman whose husband suffered a stroke and spent four months in a combination of ICU and rehab. Month after month she stood in front of her congregation and expressed how close she had grown to her Savior, how strengthened and blessed she had been to come to know Him even better through those difficult months.

You might think I'm partial to women's stories. I suppose I think of them first because we women tend to share our challenges with one another. But there are just as many men who carry their lamps for all to see. Again, it doesn't even have to be through difficult challenges. It can be through good times as well.

I think of the clerk at church who goes out of his way to post the hymn numbers for me each Sunday. (I'm the pianist.) I go to the piano, pick up my hymn book, and find that he's marked the page of the first song with the weekly bulletin. Handwritten at the top of the bulletin is a smiley face with a note from this gentleman: "Good morning, Sister Pehrson." It always makes me smile, and he probably has no idea how much this little extra brightens my Sunday mornings.

As a lamp bearer, you may find yourself moving in and out of the three roles of Light Bearing. Sometimes you may feel like an advocate, and eventually you may shift into a thought leader role. But even thought leaders are more like lamp bearers in their day-to-day interactions. For example, my children don't read my books. They don't have a clue about what I do in my business. They don't relate to the woman the world sees on Facebook or on my websites. To them, I'm "Mom." In fact, most of the people at church see me as "the piano player." In these places, my role is a Lamp Bearer.

No matter where you are in your life or what interests you pursue, each Light Bearer role is important and can change the world.

Advocates and Thought Leaders

As I've worked with thousands of people over the years, nothing frustrates me more than seeing a talented individual with an amazing story to share, but who holds it inside, afraid to let it out. When I see these individuals, I see amazing forces for good in the world. But it's all trapped behind a wall of fear, self-doubt, and anxiety.

I've found that thought leaders and advocates invariably face similar challenges. We're often afraid to mess up, afraid of embarrassment or rejection, even afraid of success. We may feel unworthy or worthless. Some people's hands may be tied simply because they do not understand the technology and systems for delivering their message. For example, how do you write that book? Get it into print? Create a product funnel? Get a website up? Get people to come to your website? Make sales?

And once you have figured all that out, there's the inevitable self-doubt and fear that even successful entrepreneurs face.

The problem for those who fail to share their messages can be summed up in this quote from Kirk Duncan: "Inspiration without expression leads to depression." As long as your message stays trapped inside you, you will never experience the pure joy and exhilaration that can be yours. On the contrary, you will feel as if you're living a life of mediocrity at best and of depression at worst.

When I look at people like this, I see an amazing force for good who can light up this world and bring peaceful unity to the planet—the likes of which hasn't been seen since the Garden of Eden.

As long as Light Bearers stay trapped behind walls of fear, self-doubt, and anxiety, we're heading for an ever darkening world. There are so many people out there, lost and alone, not sure which way to turn. And then there are people who have answers, who can show them the way to freedom. But if we don't climb up and let our lights shine like cities set on a hill, these people will continue to grope in darkness, and the world will become more lost.

This world needs more courageous Light Bearers willing to stand up with conviction, torch in hand, rallying others to the light. Most likely, you have been through your own difficult times and have found your way to freedom. You've learned important lessons. You've found solutions to the specific challenges you've faced. Those solutions can be another person's salvation!

Our natural instinct when we reach this place of newfound freedom is to turn around and lift someone else. We're so grateful and excited about what we've learned that we can't wait to help others going through the same challenges we faced. Most of us aren't satisfied to help the occasional person here or there; we want to change the world!

The problem comes when you attempt to do this and run into your own walls of self-doubt, feelings of unworthiness, fears, and anxiety. The mechanics of doing it can be daunting as you hit technology barriers and marketing learning curves that zap the enthusiasm right out of you. It all sounds great in theory, but when it comes time to take your message to the world, you may wonder if anyone even wants to hear it anymore. You might be asking yourself, "Who am I to share this? Nobody wants to listen to me."

I hope you know that where there is desire, there is power. If you have desires to serve, you are called to the work! If you have a desire to change the world, then you have the power to do it.

There are 3 steps to overcoming what feels like insurmountable challenges:

Step 1: Align yourself with your message with clarity, focus, and congruity.
Step 2: Distill your message in a way that is duplicable and purchasable.
Step 3: Get your message in front of your audience.

When you work through these steps:

1) You'll be able to influence thousands, if not hundreds of thousands, of lives for good.
2) If you wish, you'll be able to make money doing what you love.
3) You'll light up the world, changing it for the better.

So let's take each of these steps one at a time. Bear in mind that these steps are for those who wish to impact the world on a large scale with their message and create a business around it (thought leaders and advocates). I realize this isn't the goal for everyone reading this book, and that's okay.

Step 1: Align Yourself with Your Message with Clarity, Focus, and Congruity.

It's important to take the time to get clear about your message. One thing that has helped me with this is to look back on the lessons I've learned along the way. Take some time to journal about the following questions.

1. What have I learned via the "school of hard knocks?"
2. What have I learned from my successes?
3. What special training or education have I received?
4. What kinds of people do I resonate with most? What kinds of people do I enjoy working with, associating with, etc.?
5. If I could share any message with these people, what would it be? What do I want them to know?

Take some time to write these things down. Then look for patterns. Do you see a common thread throughout your life history? For example, I love working with Light Bearers. I've spent the last twenty-two years as an entrepreneur. I've overcome the fear, the self-doubts, the anxiety. I've made it through financial challenges and learned to create a great income doing what I love most—inspiring people. I've taken courses to learn how to help people align their energy with success and overcome the mind-games and self-doubts that naturally creep in when we're trying to change the world for good.

All of this comes together to serve the audience I love working with most. And the message I want my fellow Light Bearers to know is: "There are no limits to the impact for good you can have in the world. All limitations are only in your mind. Your fears are False Evidence Appearing Real. In truth, you are a glowing ball of love and light here to illuminate the path to liberty for all who resonate with you!"

Once you decide on your message, whom you serve, and how you will serve them, you'll be on your way. You will see success and you will see failures. Don't be surprised if you hit a point in your journey after you've seen a measure of success where your mettle is tested.

Step 2: Distill Your Message into a Duplicable, Purchasable Form.

If you are a thought leader who wants to influence the world on a large scale, you can't be trading hours for dollars. You can't be in front of each and every customer, working with them one-on-one. You've got to get what's in your head and heart out on paper, into courses, into audios, DVDs, and workshops. You also can't be a one-hit wonder with only one book.

You need to leverage what you know so that it can be consumed by the thousands of people who need it.

One of the easiest ways to package what you know is to have a friend or coach interview you about your area of expertise. Record the interview and have it transcribed. You can now either sell the audio and transcript or take the transcript and flesh it out into a book or course.

Step 3: Get Your Message in Front of Your Audience

I'm going to say a dirty word. Are you okay with that? It's called marketing. I'm always surprised at how many entrepreneurs have a problem with marketing. Personally, I love it. To me, marketing is just conveying my message to people in as many ways as I possibly can.

I use content to market myself and my clients. I look at it as sharing what I know in a natural, organic way. To me, it's easy, natural, and fun. After all, my message is my favorite subject! Let's say I have an epiphany about the cycles that creatives go through. I would document that epiphany in the method that was most natural to me at the time. I might record it as an audio on my phone and have it transcribed, or I might write it down. I might pull out my flip cam and shoot a video. However I'm in the mood to document it, that's where I start.

Then, I can take that documented epiphany and turn it into all kinds of things—articles, videos, press releases, a chapter in a book, an audio download, a CD, or even a DVD. I repurpose it in as many forms as I can and then use the automated marketing system I've created at IdeaMarketers.com to blast it to the world. I also leverage other popular sites like Facebook, Twitter, Pinterest, and YouTube to distribute the message.

Create once and repurpose. Each piece of content should drive people back to your website, where people can sign up for something you have to offer. For best results, offer a free gift that entices them to give you their name and email address. That way you can follow up with them over time. Eventually, they'll purchase something you have to offer.

In going through these three steps, the problems most people face are the ones in their own minds. Carolyn Cooper calls it your "energetic stance." If you're going for a goal, but deep down you don't believe it's possible or you're sabotaging it in any way, then your energetic stance is out of alignment. It's like James said in the Bible: "A double minded man is unstable in all his ways." Double-mindedness gets you nowhere. The opposing energy forces negate one another.

Here are some typical thoughts that hold people back. You're setting out to change the world or just take your business to the next level, but deep down you feel or believe:

- I'm a nobody.
- I'm not important

- Nobody wants to hear what I have to say.
- It's wrong to take money for my services.
- I'm not good enough.
- It's hard to make money.
- I'm no expert. I'd be an imposter if I claimed to be an expert, and I don't want anyone to find out.

You might be experiencing:

- scarcity thinking
- guilt or shame
- a relationship that's dragging you down
- fear of embarrassment
- fear of success

You might be wondering:

- What if I change and people don't like me anymore?
- What if I'm super successful and become proud and arrogant?
- What if my friends go away when I'm successful?
- What if I choose the wrong niche and build a business around the wrong message or audience?
- What if I'm so successful I don't have time for my family anymore?

The questions and self-doubts could go on and on. But there is a way to turn these things around, to release the negative and false beliefs and install new beliefs that are positive and productive.

When I consult with clients, I use a cutting-edge energy method to work on their energetic stance. Most people try to change their beliefs by reining in their thinking and using affirmations and visualization to reprogram the subconscious mind through repetition. Once the subsconscious mind believes something, your energy shifts and puts you into action in ways that draw what you want to you.

This method works. I've used it for over a decade, and it's still very useful to me. But there is a faster way to get down into the energy and reap results faster. Imagine your energy as a sort of computer. It's got buggy programming in it, even a few viruses. What if you could remove those buggy programs and viruses and install an upgraded operating system? What if you could install success software that knew how to reap the results you want to achieve?

With energy work, we can remove the old, ineffective, and negative programming. Then we can install new, positive beliefs and raise the vibration on good things. From there the energy starts to affect your thoughts, words, actions, habits, and results. There's no wading through the conscious and subconscious minds for months before seeing results.

Besides getting your energy stance in alignment, I can also help you navigate the second and third steps of the process: product creation, book publishing, and marketing your message to the audience who needs it. A great start is to tune in to our IdeaMarketers.TV Marketing Makeover Show, where we take a Light Bearer from idea to income and you can follow along and learn by example. I also have resources for Light Bearers at MarniePehrson.com.

7 Ways to Create a World-Changing Movement

Do you consider yourself a thought leader or tribal leader? If so, would you like to know the secret to creating a movement around your cause or message?

- Imagine 15 to 20 percent of the U.S. population loving your ideas.
- People love them so much, they turn up by the thousands wherever you go, just to hear you share your message one more time.
- When you need money to better educate the world, all you have to do is say the word and within a week or less, people have sent you millions of dollars to get it done.
- You know you can't spread your message alone, but no worries: Your followers are advocates. They willingly volunteer their time, money, and energy to spread your message to their friends. They even get online, make videos, and create blogs to talk about you and your message.

- They show up when you need them to. They volunteer because your message is so important to them that they can't sit still.
- When the world calls you crazy, your supporters go to bat for you, taking action in proactive ways.
- You and your message aren't a passing fad. People follow you year after year in ever growing numbers.

How is this possible, you ask? It must be a stroke of luck, right? In my opinion, there is no such thing as luck. Luck is when preparation meets opportunity. Much of it is about being at the right time at the right place with the right message. But there's more to it than that, and there's much we can learn about creating a movement by dissecting one in progress.

That's what I intend to do here. You don't have to agree with the person I use as the example. You don't have to support him, his movement, or believe in his cause in order to dissect what is working.

The person I speak of has very little charisma or ability to speak eloquently, yet he has made quite a stir with an avid following. It's true. You don't have to be a savvy speaker oozing charisma to create a movement! Isn't that a relief?

Movements are compelling and newsworthy, and any compelling story addresses six main elements: who, what, why, when, where, and how. I'll add one more as a bonus. So let's look at these seven characteristics of a movement. As we do, think about your own message and your own character traits. How many of these do you possess? In which areas do you need a little work?

Who: Do You Have Integrity and Engender Trust?

The "who" is Dr. Ron Paul, OB-GYN, congressman from Texas and presidential candidate. This is a man who has preached the same message for over thirty years. He's in his seventies. He stammers and stumbles over his words while delivering his message. He preaches his message in a way many might say sounds like a broken record. He's accused of being dangerous, an idealist, and a dreamer.

But there is an important take-away here: Ron Paul lives in complete alignment, in utter congruity with his message. You know what you're getting. He practices what he preaches even when it's not popular. He says the same thing to every crowd — even when people boo him. His message never wavers and his voting record never varies.

There is a sense there will be no surprises with this man. You know what you're getting and you can take his integrity to the bank.

Ask yourself, "How congruent am I with my message?" Are you consistently dependable in word and action? Is your name and reputation synonymous with your message? Do you live it vertically, horizontally, and diagonally?

What: Is Your Name Synonymous with One Compelling Message?

What is Dr. Paul's message? In one word, "liberty." Specifically, liberty in strictly following the U.S. Constitution. His is a clarion call to return to a 224-year-old document. This is a document with a track record for creating the greatest free nation in history. When it was followed strictly, it fostered freedom. When the nation veered from it, freedom diminished.

That is Ron Paul's message. It doesn't matter if he personally believes in a social agenda; if the U.S. Constitution does not give the federal government the right to rule upon or make laws about it, then Ron Paul votes against it. He'll tell you that the issue needs to be handled at an individual, state, or local level. It's not a federal matter.

What is your message? Can you relay it as succinctly as "liberty" or "Go back to the U.S. Constitution?" Or does it take more than five minutes to explain? Do you stand by your message no matter what the personal cost?

Why Do You Do What You Do?

On more than one occasion, Ron Paul has declared, "I don't want to run your life. I don't know how to run your life. I don't have the authority to run your life. And the Constitution doesn't permit me to run your life." Another time I've heard him say concerning the

Oval Office, "I just don't sit around daydreaming about it, but I'm in the race and I'm in a good race."

You get the feeling this man cares nothing for power or gain. He lives in a modest rancher-style home that looks like the one my parents purchased in the late '60s.

So why does Ron Paul do what he does? He could be retired, puttering around in his garden or playing with his grandchildren. Why does he extend himself in what many feel is a hopeless cause?

Because he cares about his country and the people in it. He loves liberty, and he wants every American to bask in it. He feels compelled to educate.

How self-serving is your message? Is it all about you and you making money? Or is it about making the world a better place and leaving a legacy? Dig down deep. What are your motives? Are they power and gain? If they are, you might be able to fool yourself, but you won't fool others for long.

When Should People Act On Your Message?

Timing is everything. And in this instance, the time is now. There is a sense of urgency to Ron Paul's message. The country is on the brink of another war and impending monetary collapse. Unemployment is rising, and people are looking outside the box for a solution that hasn't been provided by politicians in recent history.

There's also a sense that this isn't about a single election. This is a man who sees himself as a teacher, developing a movement. The youth find him enthralling. College campuses overflow when he arrives. Military personnel donate more to his campaign than they do to all the other candidates combined.

Ron Paul is encouraged by this youthful exuberance because it means that even if the adults who embrace the status quo will not accept the message, the rising generation is embracing and avidly supporting it. If the adults let America collapse, the rising generation will know what document to return to when it's time to rebuild.

Are you creating a sense of urgency around your message? Are you helping people see what will happen if they don't take action? Are you in this for the long haul, and do you have a long-term vision?

Where Is Your Message Applied?

The where is America. Ron Paul's clarion call is to concentrate on our own problems and stop fighting other people's wars or meddling in other countries' affairs. His message is to focus on protecting our own borders, building our own nation, fixing our own economic problems, supporting our own liberty, and letting other countries do the same for theirs. As Washington and Jefferson suggested, "peace, commerce, and honest friendship with all nations, entangling alliances with none."

What's your "where?" Is your message applicable on a regional, national, or global level?

How Will You Execute Your Plan?

The "how" is the U.S. Constitution. Return to it. Strictly follow it. Dr. Paul also has a plan to cut one trillion dollars from the budget in the first year in office. This plan, along with the short U.S. Constitution, is downloadable online for anyone's review.

Do you have a plan? Is it documented? How easy is it for people to find it, study it, and learn about it?

Notice how simple the message is: "liberty." Notice how simple the method is: "Strictly follow the U.S. Constitution and the founders' interpretation of it." The message is simple. Applying it seems complex, primarily because there is so much reeducation required. That complexity is what makes many say he's crazy, a dreamer, or downright dangerous.

All of this plays into the success of his movement. When a large segment of the population (or the media) calls you crazy, dangerous, or a dreamer, there is another segment of the population who will rally to your cause—especially if you're conveying a message that strikes at the deepest cravings of people's hearts.

Who doesn't want to be free? Who wants to have someone telling them every move to make? The quest for freedom is older than time itself.

How compelling and relevant is your message? Does it address a primary need of every human heart?

The freedom message strikes at the heart of every enlightened being. When that message is delivered in congruity and opposed by forces that seem bigger and stronger, there are always those who rally around to defend and support.

That brings us to bonus characteristic number seven.

Bonus: Is There Opposition?

The opposition is as important as the hero. Who would Harry Potter be without Voldemort? Who would Dorothy be without the Wicked Witch of the West? Who would Superman be without Lex Luthor? Who would Colonel Doolittle and his fly boys be without Japan? A hero is only as strong as his adversary. In our example, we have Ron Paul on one side and the establishment, the media, and the status quo on the other. That's some heavy-hitting opposition, which lends itself to the creation of a heavy-hitting hero.

Is there opposition to your message? Are there those who would say you're crazy or that your plan is impossible? Sometimes the opposition is within ourselves or our own families. It can even be nature itself. If you're not bumping up against some form of opposition, you're not being bold enough. How can you make your message clearer, bolder, stronger, and more consistent? You don't need to offend people intentionally, but if there is no opposition, there's most likely nothing rallying about your message.

In summary, ask yourself how you can live in 100 percent congruity with your message. Until you do and have a good start on these other characteristics, your quest to change the world and create a movement will most likely remain elusive.

Destined for Freedom

Pamela Stevens-Steffensen shared this story with me, and I believe it conveys wonderfully the typical Light Bearer journey — especially the exhilarating freedom that can be yours as you step into God's purpose for your life.

As I was growing up, one of our favorite family vacations was camping at Lake Powell, which is located in Southern Utah and Arizona. We would go there every summer and swim, boat, hike, catch lizards and frogs, sit around camp fires, and look at the stars. When we were old enough, we'd learn how to waterski.

I love waterskiing! To me, when I'm gliding along the water behind the boat, I feel this exhilarating rush of freedom and joy. For me, it's the closest I've ever felt to what it must be like to fly free as a bird, which is something I've always wanted to experience. When I waterski, I feel alive and free!

Well, I feel that way now about waterskiing, but it wasn't always like that. Back when I was 6 or 7 and I was trying to learn how, I didn't think it was fun at all! We went the first part of June and the water still felt cold. In order to learn, I had to go out and float in the deep water in my big, orange "Mae West" life jacket, with my head barely out the top like a turtle poking his head out of his shell. I would float in the cold water holding onto the end of the ski rope, waiting for the rope to tighten and start gently pulling me through the water. Then I would yell, "Hit It!"

You yelled, "Hit It" and the driver, which was usually my dad, did the boat equivalent of putting the pedal to the metal. This rapid acceleration is meant to pull the skier out of the water. However, for me at that tender age, the boat's acceleration only served to yank me forward onto my face, pushing water up my nose and causing me to swallow more than my fair share of lake water. (And let me tell you, that lake water can taste nasty!) After sputtering around a bit, I got to try to get up on my big, awkward waterskis again. Unfortunately, the results were almost always the same, with a variation on the theme of how much lake water I swallowed, and how much water I got up my nose! I would say, "Hit It" and get pulled onto my face time and time again, now shivering from floating so long in the water rather motionless while waiting for the boat to circle back around for me to grab the rope.

"At this point, being so young, I wanted to give up. I definitely did not want to learn how to waterski! It was too hard, too uncomfortable, and too cold! I thought waterskiing was supposed to be fun. You can imagine my horror when my dad refused to let me give up! The next day my dad was taking my oldest brother, Rick, for a ski ride. As he was leaving, Dad turned to me and said, 'When I get back from taking Rick, it's going to be your turn, Pam.' I begged and pleaded not to have to go back into the Lake for that torture, but to no avail. I knew when my dad returned in the boat, I would have to put on that uncomfortable life jacket, go sit in the cold water, and most likely drink more lake water! So I made a decision—the brilliant kind of decision that only a kid can make. I decided to hide. I thought to myself, "If my dad can't find me, he can't make me try to ski again."

The only potential problem I could see was that we were camped on a beach where there was only sage brush and our tent. So, after carefully weighing my options, I hid behind our tent, hoping he wouldn't come looking for me, and instead would concede and take someone else out waterskiing. Do you think he came and found me? You're right. He did just that. Imagine my surprise when it didn't even take him very long to figure out where I was! I was taken straight out to the cold lake in my orange life jacket. I was pulled onto my face a few more times, and then something extraordinary happened. I actually got up and stayed up. Well, at least for five or six feet. But that was enough to give me the feel of what I was trying to accomplish. After I said "Hit It" the next time, the boat really did pull me up and out of the water, and I managed to stay up for a rather long ride. My family said I was smiling so big that

I was actually beaming from ear to ear the entire time. That was the beginning of my love affair with waterskiing, and it is still going strong today.

Before too long, I was begging my dad to take me waterskiing rather than begging him to take someone else. I am the fifth of seven children, and the priority usually went to the older kids when it came to ski rides. After begging to go out again, I was frequently told I would have to wait my turn. This usually meant waiting until two or three of my older siblings had taken a turn. When it finally was my turn again, I never wanted to stop. I quickly earned a reputation in our family for taking the longest waterski rides.

Even after more than forty years, water skiing is still one of the most enjoyable and freeing activities I do. It is an activity that now bonds my own family together as we create camping and waterskiing memories of our own. My husband is an amazing waterskier, as are both of my kids. (Although my son does the wakeboard version.)

Have you ever noticed that some of the most freeing and rewarding experiences in life often come after persevering through the difficult, uncomfortable and painful ones? Thanks to my dad, that was a lesson I learned very early in life and I have never forgotten it. What if instead of making me go waterskiing, my dad had said, "Sure, Pam, you can wait until tomorrow, or the next trip, or even next year to try water skiing. Just let me know when you feel like it." Who knows how long I would have waited and how many exhilarating waterski rides I would have missed out on.

The problem is, most of us would never choose on our own to go through the pain and discomfort life can throw at us, even when it is unknowingly leading us to the freedom and joy that awaits us on the other side. How ironic that the experiences which have the potential to bring us the most growth, self-confidence, joy, and freedom, are often the very experiences which are the most painful and difficult. The ones that force us out of our comfort zones, and sometimes even cause us to fall on our faces a few times. I'm grateful my dad taught me that sometimes beautiful gifts come wrapped in an unappealing package with unattractive wrapping paper. I learned that if you don't unwrap the package, you'll never know what awaits you inside. (Pamela may be contacted at www.gpstoyoursuccess.com or pamela.stevens.steffensen@gmail.com.)

We may feel, as Pamela did, that our Heavenly Father is forcing us to endure uncomfortable and even miserable conditions. We may feel that He keeps tossing us in the icy water over and over again, insisting we learn a lesson we don't even realize is necessary. Like Pamela, we may want to run and hide from our destiny. It's too hard, too scary, and too uncomfortable. Why can't we just stay where it's warm and dry? Why can't life be easier? And what's the point? Will things really ever get better?

Our Heavenly Father knows the end from the beginning. He knows that when we finally learn that lesson and stand up on our spiritual skis, we're going to have the time of our lives. We're going to experience more freedom, more possibilities, and more exhilaration than we ever thought possible.

This is my hope for you, that you can find that place where you're a clean, clear, transparent conduit of God's love and light. There is nothing more thrilling than being an instrument in the hands of God to bless other people's lives. It's our chance to be part of His miracles on an ongoing basis.

There is nothing more liberating. This is why I've put together a special website for Light Bearers and those looking for direction.

DestinedForFreedom.com is for you.

It's for your friends, and it's a place for you to get to know other Light Bearers. You'll find tips and tools shared by thought leaders on various subjects related to finding freedom. It may be physical freedom, freedom from the past, or freedom to pursue an exciting future. It could be freedom from old generational patterns or freedom to move forward in your life.

On the site, you will also find the Destined For Freedom Facebook Group, where you can interact with other Light Bearers progressing along their journey.

I want you to know that you are not alone! Not only is God on your side, but there is a whole network of people ready to support you on your journey. Find the mentors who resonate with you. Follow their taillights along the path to the tree (the Love of God).

We're all in this together, and we're all rooting for one another.

Please stop by www.DestinedForFreedom.com and be a part of this incredible journey to shift the planet. Change IS coming. We can take this world to a Freedom Shift. We can be a part of preparing the Earth for our Savior's coming.

Let's light up the world together!

ABOUT THE AUTHOR

Marnie Pehrson is a best-selling author, speaker, certified SimplyHealed™ practitioner, and online publicist who helps Light Bearers build influential online platforms. Through her flagship site, IdeaMarketers.com, she uses innovative contextual content marketing to put your articles, press releases, information products, videos, audios and expertise in front of your ideal clients. Marnie is also a mother of six and the author of 23 fiction and nonfiction titles.

Marnie has been highlighting truth and talent online since 1996. Whether she's writing a novel that spotlights individuals who've made a difference in the world or helping a talented entrepreneur create a platform for his life's work, or giving a seminar on how to Light the World with your message, Marnie's life is about underscoring truth and talent in innovative and compelling ways.

Marnie is the founder of multi-denominational SheLovesGod.com which hosts the annual

SheLovesGod Virtual Women's Conference the 3rd week of October each year. She invites you to post your stories, poetry, articles and testimonies on **SheLovesGod.com.**

Marnie has served in many capacities within her church in presidencies of the women's, youg women's, and children's organizations, as a Sunday school teacher, seminary teacher, and pianist.

You may find out more about Marnie at **MarniePehrson.com** and be a part of the Light the World Movement at **DestinedForFreed.com** and **LightTheWorldNow.com.**

Marnie's Other Books Include:

- Trust Your Heart: Transform Your Ideas Into Income
- Trust Your Heart: Building Relationships That Build Your Business
- You're Here For A Reason: Discover & Live Your Purpose
- Lord, Are You Sure?
- You Can't Fly If You're Still Clutching the Dirt: How to Stop Worrying and Achieve Your God-Given Potential
- An Uncertain Justice
- Angel and the Enemy
- The Patriot Wore Petticoats
- Miss Humbug
- Rebecca's Reveries
- Waltzing with the Light

www.BooksByMarnie.com

RESOURCES

Not sure what your message is? Find Out!
Get the first 50 pages of "You're Here for a Reason: Discover and Live Your Purpose" FREE at http://www.iamjoyful.com/purpose

Want to watch a Light-Bearer go from idea to income so you can follow along and do the same?
Join us for the IdeaMarketers.TV Marketing Makeover Reality Show -
http://www.ideamarketers.tv

You Have a Message! Let's Get It Out There
Let Marnie step you through the process of getting your message out online:
http://ideamarketers.com/youhaveamessage/

Have a Christian Message You Want to Get Out?
Submit your stories, articles, poetry and testimonies for Free at http://www.SheLovesGod.com

Need Help Getting Your Book In Print?
Get a FREE audio on the secrets to the publishing process: traditional, vanity and self-publishing.
http://www.1chapterfree.com/global.htm

Ready to Step Into Your Greatness?
Consult with Marnie Pehrson personally. Details at http://www.marniepehrson.com/greatnessnow.php

www.ingramcontent.com/pod-product-compliance
Lightning Source LLC
Chambersburg PA
CBHW061652040426
42446CB00010B/1709